BROKEN IMAGES

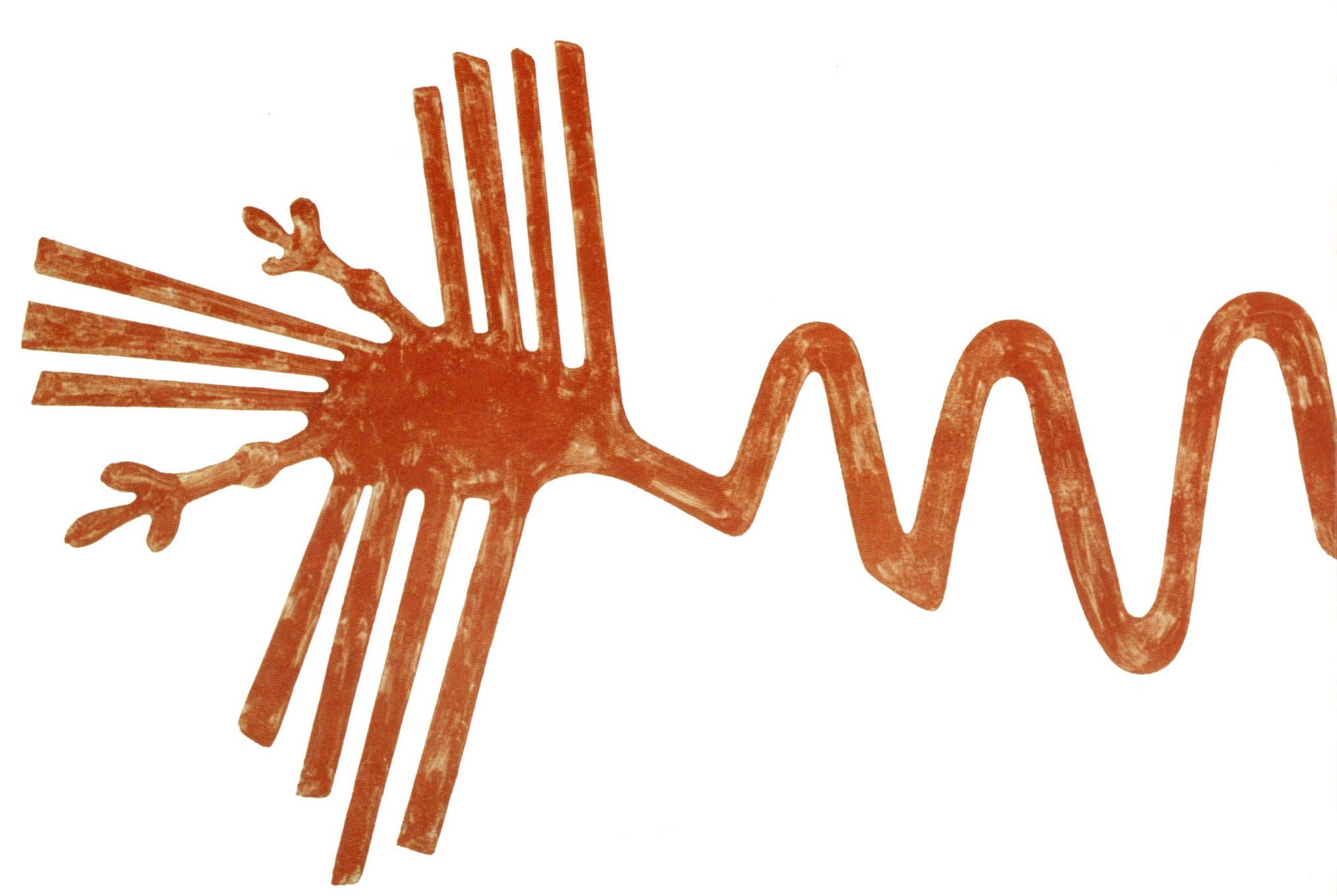

BROKEN IMAGES

THE FIGURED LANDSCAPE OF NAZCA

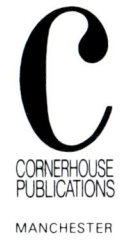

PHOTOGRAPHS BY DAVID PARKER

TEXTS BY DR HELAINE SILVERMAN & GERRY BADGER

C

CORNERHOUSE
PUBLICATIONS

MANCHESTER

for my Mother and Father

First published in 1992 by Cornerhouse Publications 70 Oxford Street,
Manchester M1 5NH. 061 228 7621

Extract from *Pathways to the Gods* (Michael Russell, Salisbury/Harper and Row,
New York) reproduced with kind permission of Tony Morrison.

Extract from *The Waste Land* by T S Eliot reproduced by permission of Faber and
Faber Ltd.

ISBN 0 948797 86 X.

Design & Art Direction: Richard Adams, AdCo Associates
Map drawing: David Parker
Typesetting: The Typesetting Business, London.

CONTENTS

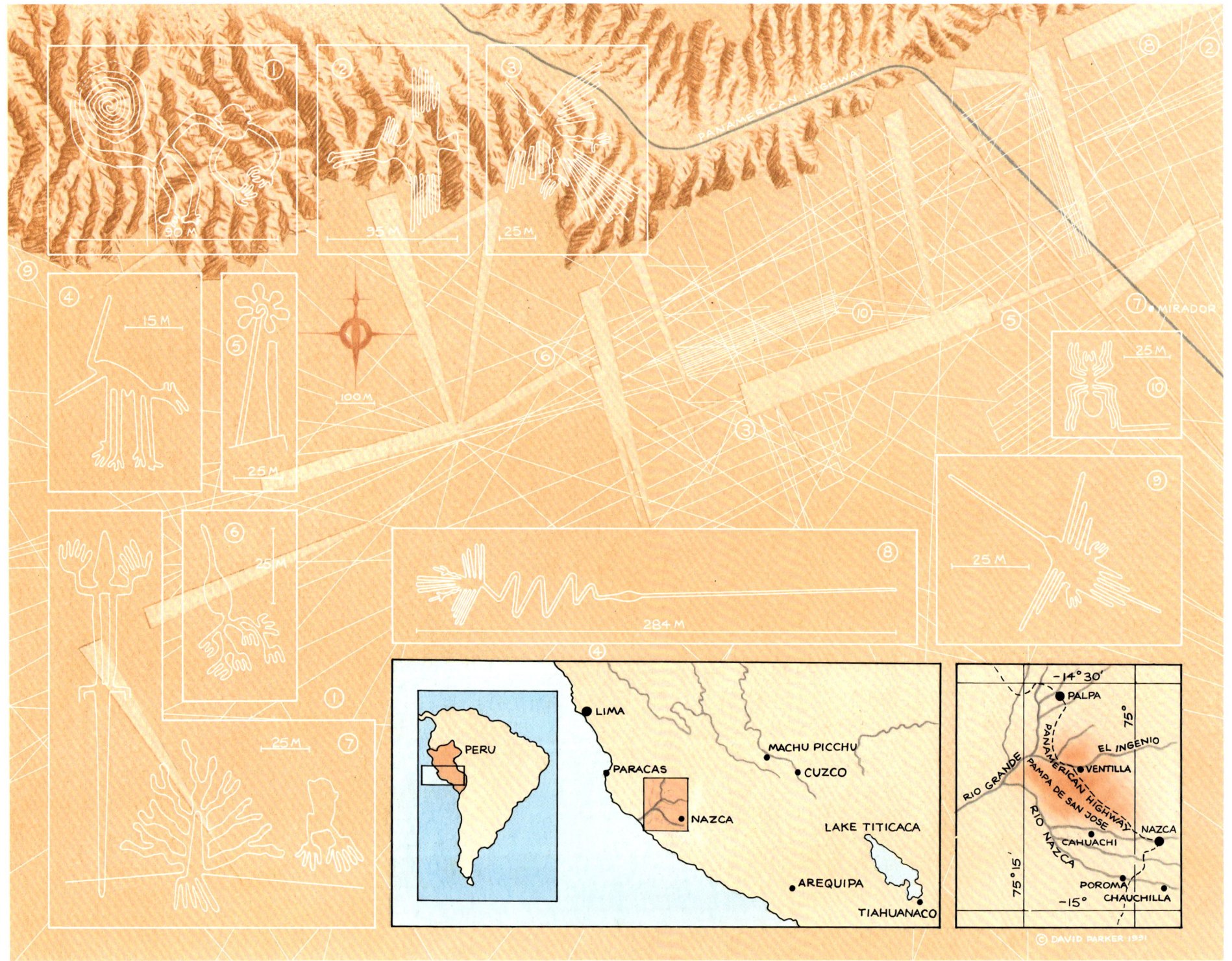

PANAMERICAN HIGHWAY

① 90 M
② 95 M
③ 25 M
④ 15 M
⑤ 25 M
⑥ 25 M
⑦ 25 M
⑧ 284 M
⑨ 25 M
⑩ 25 M

100 M

⑦ MIRADOR

LIMA
PERU
PARACAS
NAZCA
MACHU PICCHU
CUZCO
LAKE TITICACA
AREQUIPA
TIAHUANACO

-14°30'
PALPA
75°
EL INGENIO
PANAMERICAN HIGHWAY
VENTILLA
PAMPA DE SAN JOSE
RIO GRANDE
NAZCA
RIO NAZCA
CAHUACHI
75°15'
POROMA
-15°
CHAUCHILLA

© DAVID PARKER 1991

LATE ONE AFTERNOON IN 1927 a young Peruvian archaeologist, Toribio Mejía Xesspe, climbed a rocky hill overlooking the elevated desert plain (or *pampa* as it is known in Spanish) that lies between the Ingenio and Nazca valleys on the south coast of Peru. As he surveyed the arid landscape he was astounded to see a vast maze of lines stretching across the flat expanse.

Mejía Xesspe speculated that the straight, zig-zag, and furrow-like lines etched on the pampa were pre-Columbian ceremonial or religious roads and associated them with the ancient system of underground canals and prehispanic cemeteries he had already discovered in the region. Despite this fascinating interpretation, interest in the geoglyphs, as the great ground markings have come to be known, was slow to develop.

In the early summer of 1941 the fate of the desert markings was changed forever by Paul Kosok, an American geographer and historian. While on the pampa at dusk on June 21, 1941 Kosok observed the sun setting at the end of a line. With a quick interpretive leap it occurred to him that the lines might have an astronomical purpose with some lines marking solsticial positions of the sun and others pointing to the Pleiades. In his magnum opus, *Life, Land and Water in Ancient Peru* (1965), Kosok called the pampa "the world's largest astronomy book."

Kosok's theory profoundly inspired a young German teacher of mathematics, Maria Reiche, who became his disciple. For more than forty years — most of her adult life — Reiche has devoted herself to recording and protecting the fragile and enigmatic testament etched on the pampa. She has painstakingly mapped hundreds of lines and dozens of figures and determined the simple technology with which the great figures and lines were traced on the desert surface.

Reiche's primary concern has always been to elucidate the mathematical and astronomical relationships of the lines. Like her mentor, she argues that the lines marked solstices, stars, and significant positions of the sun and moon, and that the lines and their directions could have served as an agricultural calendar. Unlike Kosok, however, Reiche is ambivalent towards the prehistoric ruins of the region that provide the vibrant, changing human context for the

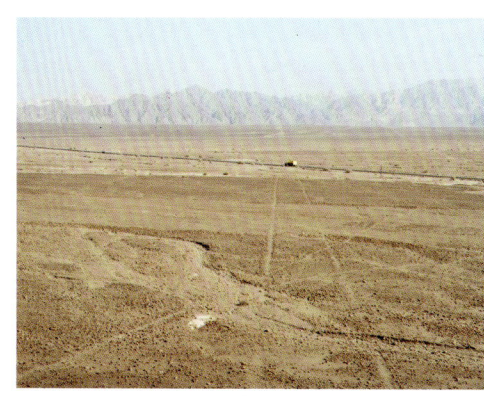

LINES CROSSING PANAMERICAN HIGHWAY

lines. Reiche has felt that the only knowledge that can possibly be retrieved from the pampa are the dimensions and angles of the lines and figures. Her exclusively astronomical interpretation has sterilised the phenomenon of the pampa, making it a mathematical, almost cabalistic, problem. Unfortunately, this has left the lines open to wild speculation by others, most notably Erich Von Daniken who has proposed that the lines were created by and for extraterrestrial visitors to Nazca (see *Chariots of the Gods?*, 1970).

By the late 1970's Reiche had become a folk hero in Peru - truly a national treasure — and nowhere more so than in the bustling coastal town of Nazca. This remarkable woman has succeeded in preserving the pampa's markings by donating the funds with which an observation tower (the *mirador*) was built along the Pan-American Highway and establishing a corps of guardians (paid from the proceeds of her book sales) who patrol the pampa's edge, protecting it from incursion. Today, a small number of Nazca's 30,000 inhabitants earn their living from the tourist industry that has grown up around the pampa phenomenon. The tourist dollars brought in from abroad are an important part of Peru's small gross national product. In gratitude the Peruvian government has given Maria Reiche room and board in perpetuity at the lovely state tourist hotel in Nazca. At first Maria gave nightly lectures in exchange for this favour but, as her health began to fail, the arrangement was soon free of any encumbrance. National and international newpapers, magazines, and documentary film-makers still court her. In Nazca, a street and a school bear her name and her birthday on May 15th has became a yearly holiday lauded with parades and speeches by the municipal authorities.

For decades no archaeologists worked on the pampa or in the valleys below it. In their absence it was Maria Reiche, rather than the Archaeological Commission of Peru's National Institute of Culture (the I.N.C.), who came to control access to the pampa. It was inevitable, however, that archaeologists would not be content with the tourist-oriented paliatives offered by the mirador and a booming aerial flight business. As archaeological work resumed in the Nazca region in the early 1980's archaeologists-national and foreign — became increasingly eager to inspect the pampa for clues about the ancient peoples who had lived in the desert oasis below. Reiche has not welcomed their interest. To her, every footprint on the pampa — even that of the most well-meaning archaeologist — threatens the preservation of the shallow etchings. To the archaeologists, Reiche is an obstacle to scientific investigation and for years archaeologists have found it almost impossible to get permission to work on the pampa because the national government has not wanted to oppose the popular Maria Reiche.

Pressured by age, Parkinson's disease, and archaeologists, Reiche searched for a successor, someone to validate and carry on her research. Reiche found such a person in astronomer Phyllis Pitluga of the Adler Planetarium in Chicago. After five seasons of work on the pampa, Pitluga has concluded that Reiche's basic conclusions are sound and that the pampa could have served the ancient Nasca people as an observatory for determining time cycles. Pitluga hopes to publish the data in support of her theory in the near future.

But not all astronomers are in agreement with Kosok, Reiche, and Pitluga. In 1968, following his 'decoding' of Stonehenge's astronomical alignments, astronomer Gerald Hawkins came to Peru to study the Nazca lines. He was granted permission to work on the pampa and chose an edge above the Ingenio Valley where the greatest concentration of geoglyphs is found. Within a 2000 × 5 metre strip he compared the alignments of 21 trapezoids and 72 other lineal features with the risings and settings of celestial objects. Using a modified version of the computer programme he had designed for Stonehenge, Hawkins was unable to demonstrate much more than a random pattern of coincidences between lines and stars. He concluded that the probability of an astronomical significance was only slightly greater than chance.

British author and film-maker Tony Morrison, who worked with Gerald Hawkins, continued to be fascinated by the problem of the Nazca lines. Morrison was not content merely to accept the disproof of Reiche's theory. If the lines were not astronomical, then what were they? To answer this question, Morrison returned to Peru and travelled the length and breadth of the Andes,

interviewing a wide range of anthropologists, archaeologists and historians. He even journeyed to midwestern Urbana, Illinois to speak with my colleague, Tom Zuidema, world expert on the Inca *ceque* system (a unified social, ritual, political, calendrical, and astronomical order that was mapped onto the Andean social, ecological and political landscape and conceived by means of imaginary straight lines radiating out from a centre point).

The more Morrison probed, the more convinced he became that the lines could best be understood as *ceques* in the broadest sense of this Andean concept: straight lines, shrines, sacred places, religious paths, and ritual calendars. Morrison published this interpretation in his outstanding 1977 synthesis of the various explanatory theories then current, together with results from original exploration in Bolivia, *Pathways to the Gods. The Mystery of the Andes Lines*. Morrison's book concludes with the observations of Luis de Monzón, the Spanish magistrate who, in 1586, asked the Indians about worked stones and traces of ancient roads not far from present-day Nazca:

'The old Indians say that, by hearsay, they have knowledge of their ancestors, that in very old times, before the Inca came to rule over them, there came to the land another people they call Viracochas, not many of them, and they were followed by Indians who came after them listening to their word, and now the Indians say they must have been saintly persons. And to them they built paths which can be seen today.'

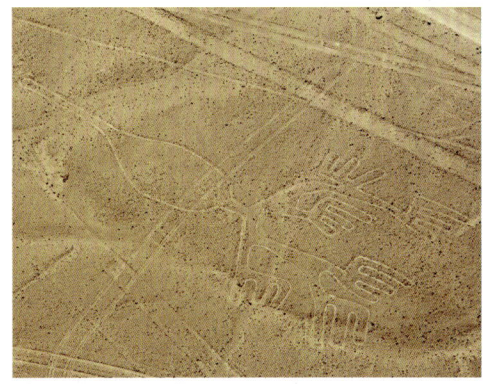

SEAWEED

Between 1981-1984 the pampa was subjected to an even more meticulous scrutiny by astronomer Anthony Aveni and anthropologist Gary Urton, both of Colgate University, and their inter-disciplinary team (see *The Lines of Nazca*, 1990).

With permission from Peru's I.N.C., the project concentrated on the spoke-like clusters of lines that dominate the pampa. A total of 741 lines, 62 line centres, and 250 trapezoids were measured; this is an incomparable data base. Analysis of these data revealed that there is a strong correlation between the lines and the points at which water occurs on the pampa together with the direction in which water moves and that there is a physical similarity of the line centres to the Inca ceque system. No significant astronomical orientations on the pampa were discovered.

Adding detail to the emerging consensus among Andeanists is anthropologist Johan Reinhard. Reinhard has carried out a major comparative study of geoglyphs throughout the Andes. Many are known in northern Chile and Bolivia and, although none compares to the complexity of the Nazca pampa, Reinhard's archaeological, ethnohistoric and, especially, ethnographic data strongly suggest that such geoglyphs are part of the same phenomenon – a widespread ancient religious complex designed primarily to ensure crop fertility. Reinhard's culturally relevant theory is compatible with Aveni's, Morrison's, and my interpretations of the date and function of the geoglyphs and enriches them.

As an archaeologist I have long been concerned with the human and societal context of the geoglyphs. In 1988-1989 I directed the first archaeological project aimed at elucidating the geoglyphs from an extra-pampa perspective. My project identified more than 500 archaeological sites in the Ingenio and middle Grande valleys beneath the pampa. These sites cover a time span of two thousand years, from approximately 500 B.C. to the early colonial period; they range from tiny farming hamlets to immense urban centres and include some 70 new geoglyph sites ranging from simple lines to great complexes of lines, spirals, zig-zags, trapezoids, and cleared quadrangular fields.

Identifiable broken pottery found on the surface of the valley geoglyphs and the geoglyphs' association with nearby archaeological sites provide information on their date and function. Of those geoglyphs that could be dated, almost all are Nasca (ca. A.D. 1-700); very few geoglyphs appear to date to the late or post-Nasca period. Although we did not observe on the valley hillsides any of the immense figures that decorate the pampa, the lineal geoglyphs we discovered were made by the same subtractive technology as the markings of the pampa. It has been clear since publication of aerial photographs in 1944 that the figures (less than 50 in number and mostly restricted to that 5% of the pampa directly above the south side of the Ingenio

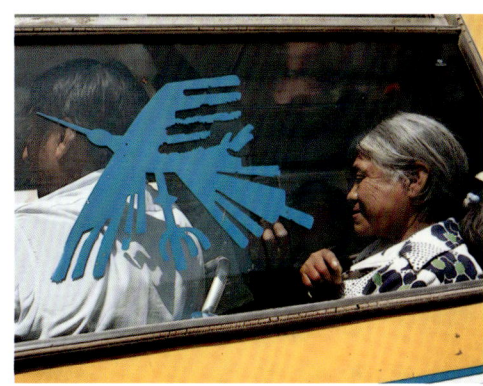

MINIBUS WINDOW

Valley at San José) are identical to the images on Nasca polychrome painted pottery suggesting that they too date to that period. Therefore, we conclude that the lines and figures of the pampa and the lines of the valleys were contemporary and were the product of an archaeological culture known as Nasca (written ʃ to distinguish it from the geographical region and modern town).

The basis of Nasca society was efficient agricultural production, reliant upon a system of water management which, in some valleys, made use of the ingenious system of underground canals reported by Mejía Xesspe. The extreme aridity of the Nazca region belies its great fertility; with adequate water all land can be made to produce, even the pampa. Indeed, the improvement and industrialisation of the region's irrigation technology represents a real threat to the survival of the geoglyphs. Just three years ago an agricultural cooperative on the north side of the Nazca Valley expanded its irrigation canal system and 'reclaimed' an edge of the pampa. The cooperative was persuaded to halt its irrigation project, but not before damage to a trapezoid had been done.

Ancient Nasca society appears to have been directed from two capitals: a monumental religious center at Cahuachi in the Nazca valley, where I excavated in 1984-1985, and a densely agglutinated urban settlement called Ventilla that was discovered in the Ingenio Valley during the recent survey. Cahuachi and Ventilla sit across from each other on opposite sides of the pampa and are directly beneath it. They were connected by a major trans-pampa line running more than twelve kilometres over the flat terrain.

Mejía Xesspe was quite right in characterising the lines as ceremonial roads for now we know that Cahuachi was a great pilgrimage centre and that many of the pampa's lines were related to religious activity, with some leading directly to the site. The name 'Cahuachi' itself is suggestive, for it derives from a Quechua word meaning 'to make them see, to make them observe, to predict, to have bad luck.' Perhaps the name recalls Cahuachi's past function as the major ceremonial focus of the Nasca people. But Cahuachi was not the only ceremonial site in the Nazca region; other, smaller ceremonial centres have been discovered. Furthermore, the marked pampa itself was an integral part

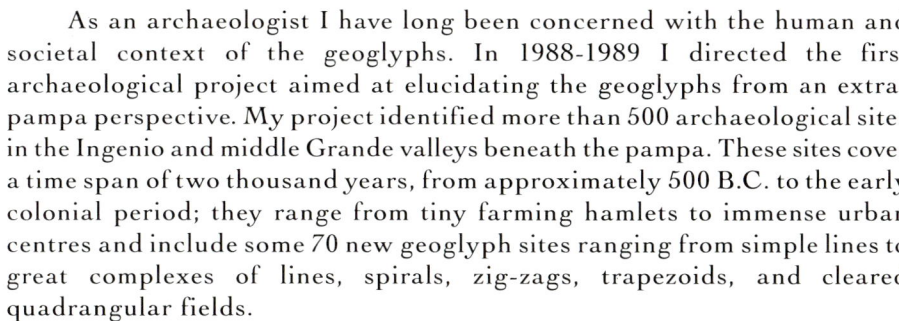

of Nasca religious space and throughout the Río Grande de Nazca drainage geoglyphs were traced on the valley hillsides.

I believe that the thousands of lines now covering the pampa's surface are the result of rituals repeated over many years. A Nasca social group would have gone to the pampa, traced a geoglyph, maintained it over a period of time and then, eventually, ceased to use it. Other Nasca groups did the same. Over the course of hundreds of years the pampa's surface became filled with the maze of lines we see today. While unique environmental conditions have acted to preserve all these ritual actions, the superposition of geoglyphs on the surface of the pampa argues forcefully for their inherent transience and cyclicity.

The geoglyphs represent no great investment of time and labour. In 1977 a Nazca school teacher and archaeology buff, Señor Josué Lancho Rojas, and his fourth-grade students made a perfectly good line, 17 ½ yards long, in half an hour for Tony Morrison's BBC film crew. In June 1984 Aveni and his twelve Earthwatch volunteers made a detailed examination of an ancient spiral. They determined that the geoglyph makers had linked together straight lines and arcs of circles by means of cords attached to two rock cairn centres of curvature (some of these rock cairns still remain) or wood stakes. Thus, neither a complex technology nor a sophisticated knowledge of geometry was required to construct a geoglyph. In antiquity the large scale of other figures and geometric markings was probably achieved by the amplification of a design following principles already present in the gridded warps and wefts of ancient Nazca textiles. All that was needed were rocks or wooden sticks to scrape with, wooden stakes, a sighting stick, cotton string, leafy branches to be used as brooms and human labour. With template and these simple tools in hand a work team could have easily broken the hard brown desert pavement, revealing a lighter coloured substratum of soil. The pebbles and small rocks covering the pampa would have been swept and lifted to the outside of the light cleared area, forming a permanent border of darker coloured rocks. When in use, the geoglyphs were bright and clear. Once abandoned, they became dulled as they filled with tiny, wind-born pebbles. Even as the pampa

filled with geoglyphs, the ancient people still could have navigated their way through the growing maze of lines since current lines would have stood out brightly on the desert pavement in contrast to those that were no longer being maintained.

The geoglyphs are a major ideological manifestation of the ancient Peruvian world. They encompassed religious, social, and political phenomena. The pampa played a role of great importance as a route of communication and pilgrimage between the great Nasca ceremonial centre of Cahuachi and other sites in the valleys on the north and west sides of the pampa, not the least of which was the Nasca urban centre of Ventilla. Together, the pampa and Cahuachi formed a centre of gravity and an irruption of the sacred on the south coast. The tracing of lines on the empty pampa surface brought it within the human sphere, domesticated it, so to speak. The pampa thus ceased to be a physical no-man's land and obstacle to be crossed to reach Cahuachi and other sites. Instead, it became a pilgrimage route and an integral part of Nasca religion.

While crossing the pampa, pilgrims entered the liminal phase that transformed them from ordinary people into ritual social beings. Analysis of Andean practices today supports Nasca iconographic evidence and suggests that this transformation was achieved by dressing up, dancing, trancing, and masking. Through the media of percussion, panpipe music and dance, pilgrims

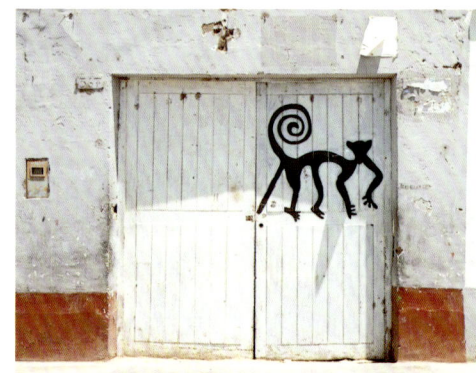

GARAGE DOOR

then, as now, must have transformed the landscape as they traversed it. As anthropologist Michael Sallnow observed at the contemporary Qoyllur R'iti pilgrimage near Cuzco (*Pilgrims of the Andes,* 1987), passive, physical features and locations were culturally appropriated and transformed into a continuous sacred topography; dance served as a formal, kinesthetic mapping of space, a living ceque system.

Archaeologists now feel confident as to who made the geoglyphs, when, and, to some extent, why. At the same time, we cannot ignore the inherent aesthetic appeal of the magnificent geometric geoglyphs. They are major works of landscape art as seen in Marilyn Bridges' extraordinary black and white portfolio (*Markings,* 1986). Nor are the geoglyphs the only such sacred landscapes created by the Nasca people. Throughout the valleys and most notably at Cahuachi, the ancient Nascas deliberately accentuated naturally terraced hillsides by means of artificial levelling and by adding mud brick walls to create truncated pyramid mounds and flat-topped hills. Together the pyramids and geoglyphs were *huacas* — the Quechua word for sacred shrines.

Although the precise messages encoded in the Nazca landscape have been lost, the geoglyphs communicate across the centuries. Taken in conjunction with the great ceremonial centre at Cahuachi, the newly discovered urban settlement at Ventilla, and the rich supernatural iconography of Nasca art, the geoglyphs provide evidence of an ancient society whose politics were clothed in ritual and whose geography was sacred.

Yet this is not the message that most tourists seek or want to hear when they come to Nazca. In my experience, the average tourist wants to look at the lines without being provided with any extra information about their archaeological and cultural setting, so that they remain a mystery. Among the abundant tourist paraphernelia one can buy at Nazca are buttons that say "I was in the past at Nazca," silk-screened T-shirts bearing images of the pampa with the logo "Mystery of the Pampa," tuna-fish sized cans with attractive blue labels bearing yellow pampa images that purport their content to be "Cosmic Air of the Pampa of Nazca," and a variety of books with titles such as *Nazca: Journey to the Sun* (1977), *The Astronomer of Nazca* (1988), *Geoglyphs of Nasca: New Designs, New Enigmas* (1985) and *Chariots of the Gods?* (1970) among others. Even Maria Reiche's book shares in this hype with its trilingual title of *Geheimnis der Wüste/Mystery on the desert/Secreto de la pampa* (1968).

The state and informal sector tourist industry are all too willing to oblige the tourist, for it is this emotional appeal of the "exotic," "unknown," "unexplained" and "unexplainable" that draws tourists in the tens of thousands to Nazca. Yet it would be relatively easy to put the geoglyphs in context by promoting tourism to some of the other monuments made by the linemakers. This would also give tourists the opportunity to walk about and appreciate archeological sites from the ground, the perspective from which they were designed and seen in ancient times. But little effort is made to do

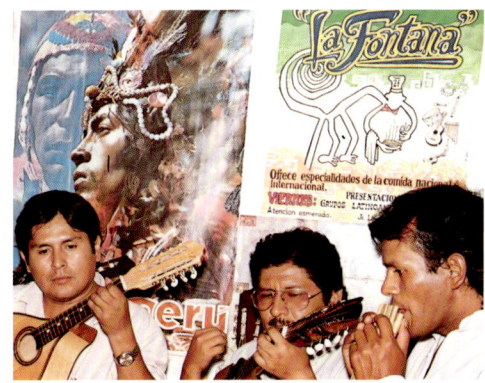

MONKEY AS WAITER

this. Instead, each tourist is encouraged to experience the geoglyphs individually and so feels like the discoverer of an enigma. While I would be the last to deny anyone their pleasure of personal discovery (I feel like an explorer each time I encounter an ancient site) it has to be said that out of context the Nazca lines do lend themselves to a very particular kind of disembodiment since, to protect them, they can only be appreciated from the air. After the nausea of the bumpy flight has passed and one regains one's humour and perspective, the successful tourist feels like a member of an exclusive clique — he or she has seen something that the vast majority of the populace has not. He or she has communed with a greater presence and, indeed, is even presented with a certificate to prove it.

To many tourists, it seems impossible that the ancestors of the native Peruvians could have created something as vast in scale as the geoglyphs. This attitude is not restricted to the Nazca lines. Be it megalithic Inca stonework, the pyramids of Egypt, or the colossal Easter Island statues, the public is all too willing to deny modern third-world peoples their past glory. This view is simply misinformed and it relegates the Nazca lines to the permanent status of mystery or, worse still, to another order of prime movers: extraterrestrial beings. Beginning with *Chariots of the Gods?* a fairly constant stream of best-selling, spectacularist theories has been put forward to explain the giant markings on the Nazca desert plain. Such theories persist in the face of an overwhelming body of scientific information to the contrary and are part of the whole "New Age" cult phenomena.

With Kosok's effective discovery of the geoglyphs in 1941 and the popularising of the pampa that has developed over the years, the status of the Nazca lines changed. From Peru's undisclosed archaeological patrimony they became the world's property — subject to analysis and discourse by all and profit-making commercialisation by a lucky few. The owners of the largest airline that flies tourists over the lines have become millionaires. They own an excellent restaurant in town and operate a fine hotel as do the owners of the two smaller airlines. Other, more modest hotels, independent of the airlines, have also sprung up. A slew of hole-in-the-wall tourist shops have opened over the past five years and local guides now abound.

Just as the ancient Nascas trekked across many of the pampa's lines on pilgrimage to and from Cahuachi, so hordes of modern tourists, some as famous as actress Shirley MacLaine (*Out On A Limb,* 1983), make their own pilgrimages to Nazca to commune with nature and the gods. Recently, tours emphasizing Peruvian native medicine and hallucinogenic drugs have begun to incorporate Nazca in their itinerary. Famous Peruvian healers, such as Eduardo Calderón, now travel regularly to the Nazca desert with their foreign clientele to produce a tourist version of shamanistic curing ceremonies, including ingestion of the mildly hallucinogenic San Pedro cactus. The credibility of these tours was greatly increased in 1987 when Maria Reiche participated in such a healing session for a television documentary.

Indeed, even Maria Reiche is an object of pilgrimage for no visit to Nazca would be complete without seeing her. She is part of the mystique of the Nazca lines and one must wonder if the popular media will seek someone else to replace her. The mythification of Maria reached its most ironic and problematic proportions when in 1989, a group of Nazca citizens decided that Reiche herself be immortalised on the pampa, preserved for posterity and visible to all who flew over. A small team of workmen was put to work clearing a small area of the pampa where it was contended no geoglyphs were located and Maria's face could be etched at ancient scale. When the municipal project came to the attention of the I.N.C. Inspector of Archaeological Monuments, he stipulated that the project should be stopped inasmuch as the whole pampa has been declared an "untouchable national reserve." He demonstrated, moreover, that there were geoglyphs on that spot as there would be anywhere on the pampa.

Maria needed no such monument on the pampa. Her place in the annals of Nazca history is secure. And whether her theory is ultimately proven right or wrong, the tourist industry of the pampa can be expected to continue. It will be unaffected by the scholars' debate although Peru's current political problems are having a temporarily negative impact. What is of more concern to me is the management of tourism in Nazca and its effect on the local populace.

On any day scores of wealthy (by Peruvian

standards) foreign tourists walk around town after their morning flight. They are subject to frequent cat-calls by the young populace, are dogged by the local tour guides, and are victims of frequent street theft. This is because Nazca, as a whole, has benefitted unequally from the town's incorporation into the national tourist industry.

It was only recently that the Nazca City Council was able to enact a tax on tourists and the local airlines so that a miniscule fraction of the millions of U.S. dollars (the preferred foreign currency in Peru) that pass through a limited number of hands in Nazca would go to help the community. Most of the advances I have seen in Nazca are cosmetic. The tourist and airline tax has enabled Nazca to erect a new city building and improve the entry to town; there is also more employment because of tourism. But — and this is as much due to the dire economic and political crisis afflicting Peru as it is to the anarchy of Nazca's management of tourism — Nazca, like any other Peruvian town, still lacks major infrastructural development. The conditions of schools, hospital, post office, telephone, water supply, housing and other facilities in Nazca are still very much on a rudimentary level.

In Nazca the discrepancy between the underdeveloped and developed world is especially pronounced since Nazca is thrust daily into contact with the outside and outsiders. Tourism is now understood by anthropologists as a particularly complex communicative system with messages running both ways — from the touring to the toured and back again. But Nazca's tourism is selective and has led to an almost total disjunction of subject and object, past and present, foreign and national, wealthy and poor. The vast majority of local residents have never seen the geoglyphs from the air but eagerly and enviously stand at the gates of the local airport watching an endless progression of camera-toting, ostentatiously dressed tourists ascend and descend the fleet of gleaming white propeller planes. The columnar monument outside Nazca's Old City Hall is adorned with a Nasca supernatural motif; the facade of the new municipality building is decorated with images from the pampa; and the pampa "Hummingbird" figure is the emblem of a major national bank. There are no traditional crafts in Nazca, only kitschy souvenirs. All images are

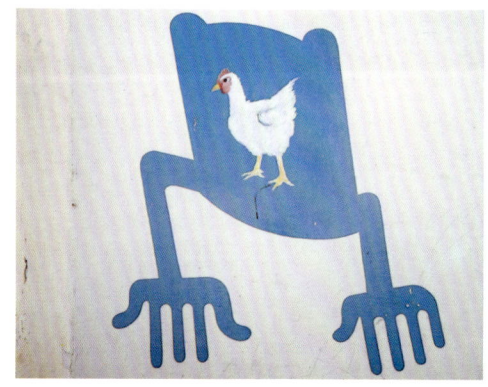

LOGO OF CHICKENFEED COMPANY

epigonalized, in the sense that they are copies of motifs made without comprehension because their meaning has been lost – truly "broken images."

Nazca is a *criollo* (coastal) and *mestizo* (mixed Indian and Spanish parentage) town. Its people struggle to eke out a daily living in this hyper-inflated country; they show little affinity with the great civilizations that once thrived in this region. Rather, the past is perceived as something to be manipulated or used for one's own direct economic benefit – whether this takes the form of looting ancient tombs for the illicit sale of grave goods to the antiquities market, charging tourists, taxied in a rickety car, to see the remains of the ancient mummified dead arranged in a macabre tableaux, or converting a wing of one's home into a hostel. The social structure of the modern Peruvian nation-state is such that the path to future success necessitates abjuration of one's non-European past.

It is with this perspective of the past and present, of tourist comment versus scientific discourse, that I find David Parker's images so compelling. He has movingly captured the other, contradictory and contested side of the pampa and the Nazca lines. He has seen and understood Nazca in very different terms to those tourists who experience Nazca as a day-trip en route to Machu Picchu. To most tourists Nazca- the town and its people-is invisible; their interest devolves completely on a single remnant or time-slice of ancient society. They are unaware of, or deliberately avoid being concerned with, the cultural, ethnic and racial continuity between those whose works they admire so much from the air and those who carry their bags. Indeed, this is an attitude promulgated by the national government itself for, as anthropologist Julian

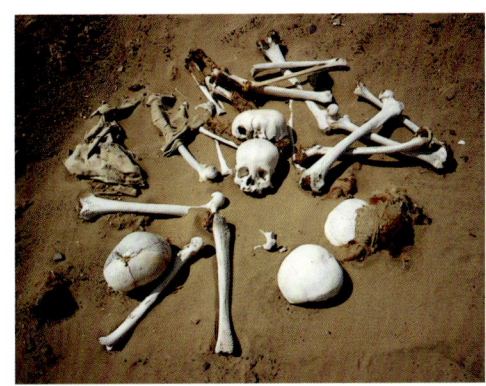

POROMA CEMETERY

Pitt-Rivers so aptly observed,

"... the place of the noble savage is on a pedestal rather than in the market-place where his nobility is soon brought into question, and the less the figure on the pedestal resembles the reality of everyday life, the more convincing his message. Tribute to the pristine forebears must not be permitted to interfere with treatment of their descendants.... the Indian can only be acclaimed at the level where he does not exist..." ("Who Are The Indians?" *Encounter* XXV, 1965).

Concomitantly, for most of Nazca's inhabitants, the pampa is a foreign phenomenon in their midst. The distance that separates them culturally from the linemakers is as great as the divide between them and their visitors. The pampa is wilfully used and misused by a variety of players in contemporary Nazca, but it is rarely understood. Archaeologists are not without blame in this ongoing process for we should make our research results equally accessible to the Peruvian people, to the general public, and to our educated professional audience. That is why, as an archaeologist with many years of research and residence in Nazca, I welcomed the opportunity to write an introduction to *Broken Images* after meeting David Parker in 1988. The cultural processes David Parker has profoundly captured on film address fundamental issues of ethnic and cultural identity, cultural change, acculturation, economic development, and dependency relations. As such these "broken images" are relevant to us all.

Helaine Silverman. 1991

What are the roots that clutch, what branches grow

Out of this stony rubbish? Son of man,

You cannot say, or guess, for you know only

A heap of broken images, where the sun beats,

And the dead tree gives no shelter, the cricket no relief,

And the dry stone no sound of water. Only

There is shadow under this red rock,

(Come in under the shadow of this red rock),

And I will show you something different from either

Your shadow at morning striding behind you

Or your shadow at evening rising to meet you;

I will show you fear in a handful of dust.

from *The Waste Land* by T S Eliot

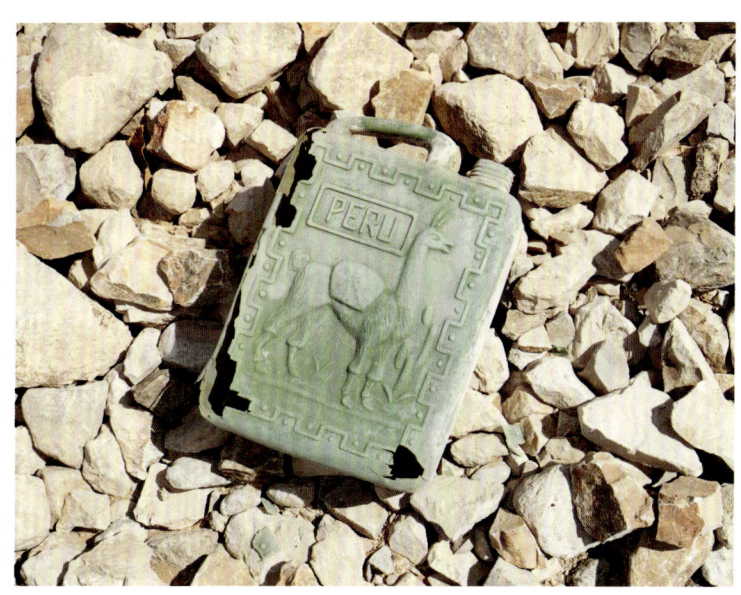

1 • KEROSENE CAN, FRONT

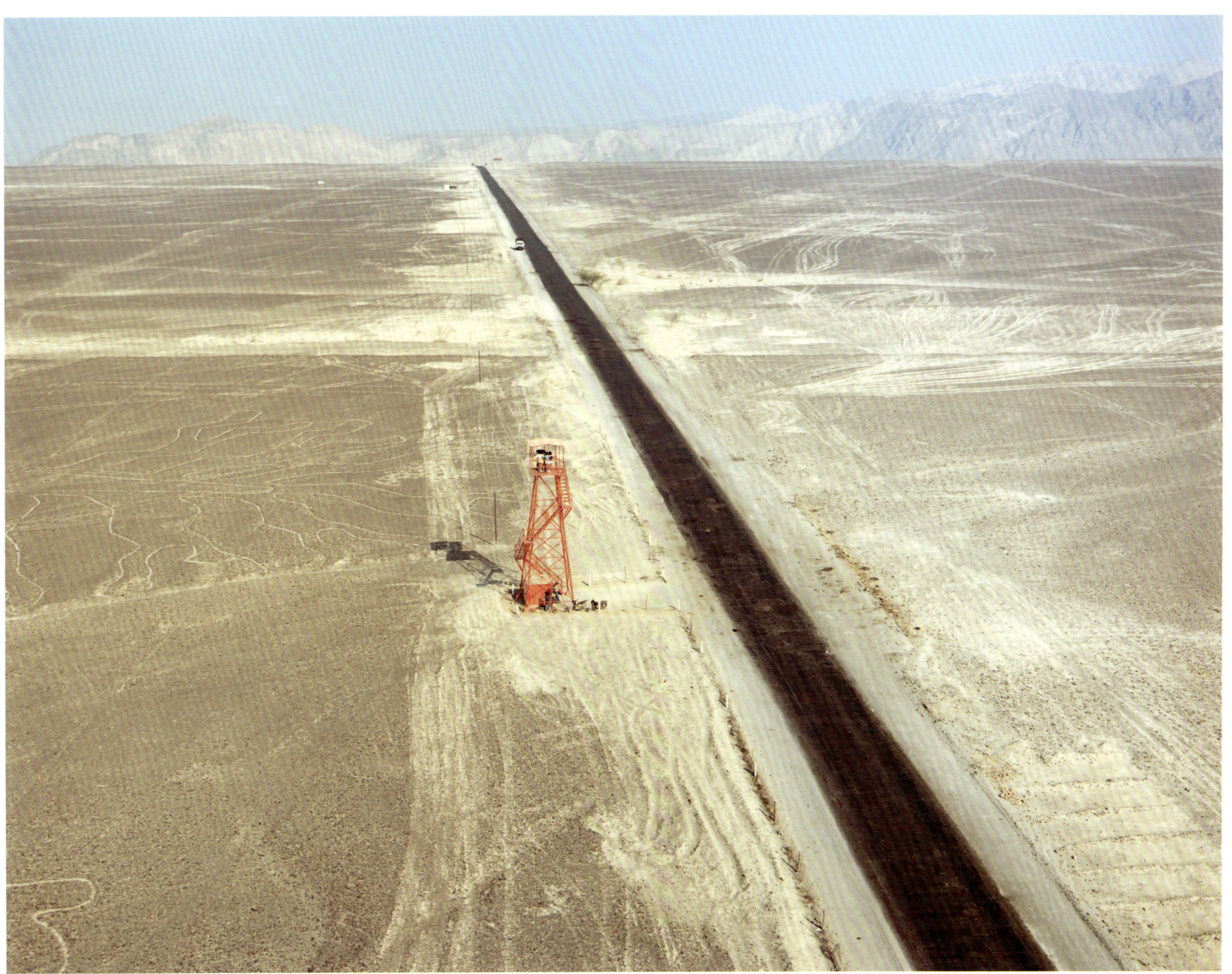

2 • PANAMERICAN HIGHWAY & 'MIRADOR'

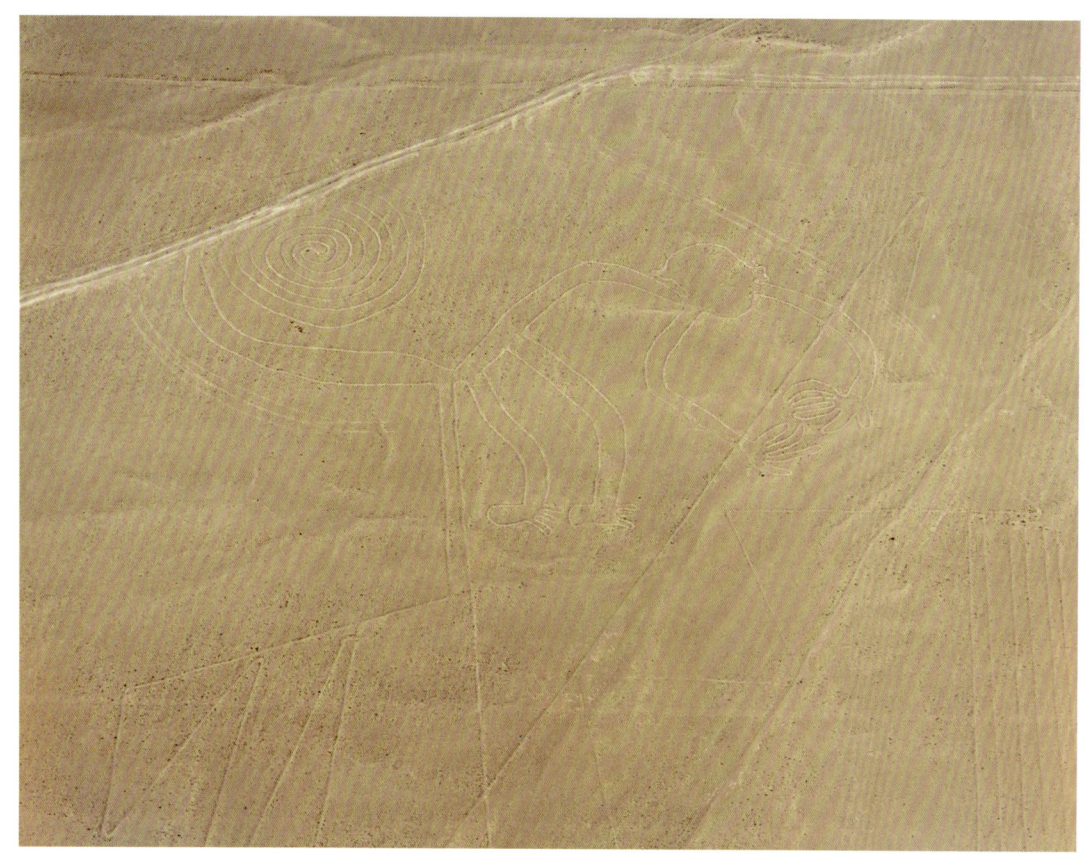

3 • Monkey & Lines

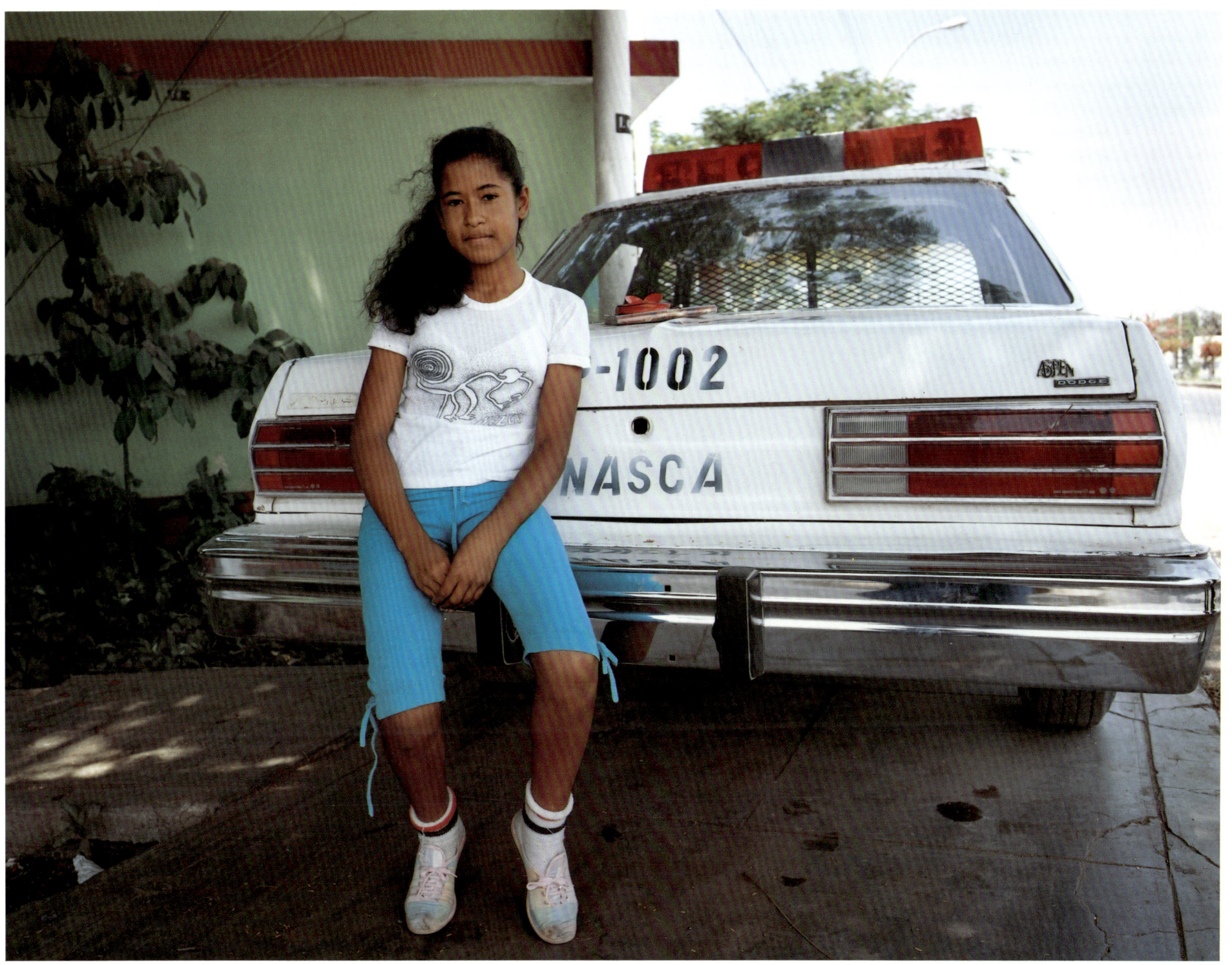

4 • POLICE STATION

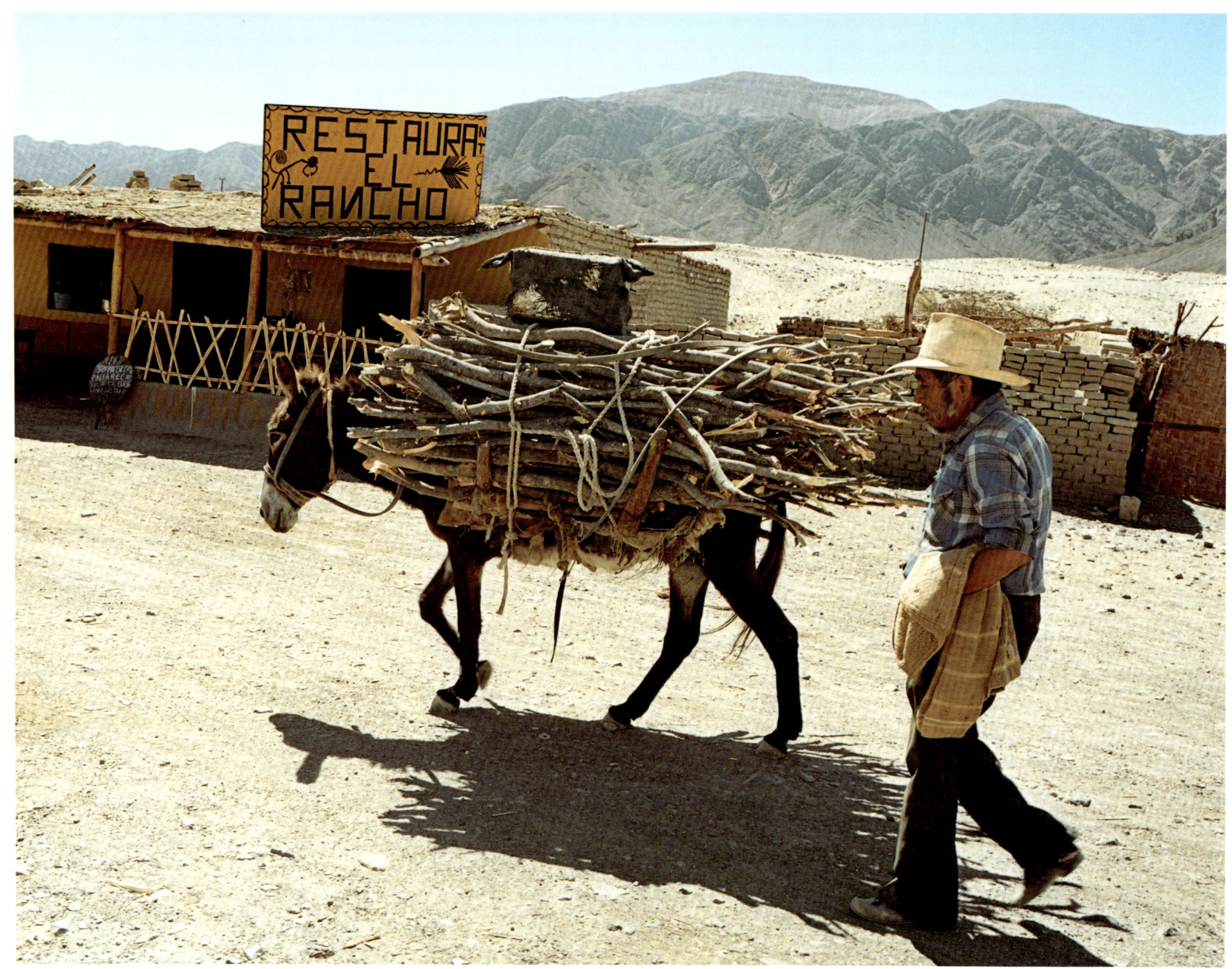

5 • PANAMERICANA TRUCKSTOP, VISTA ALEGRE

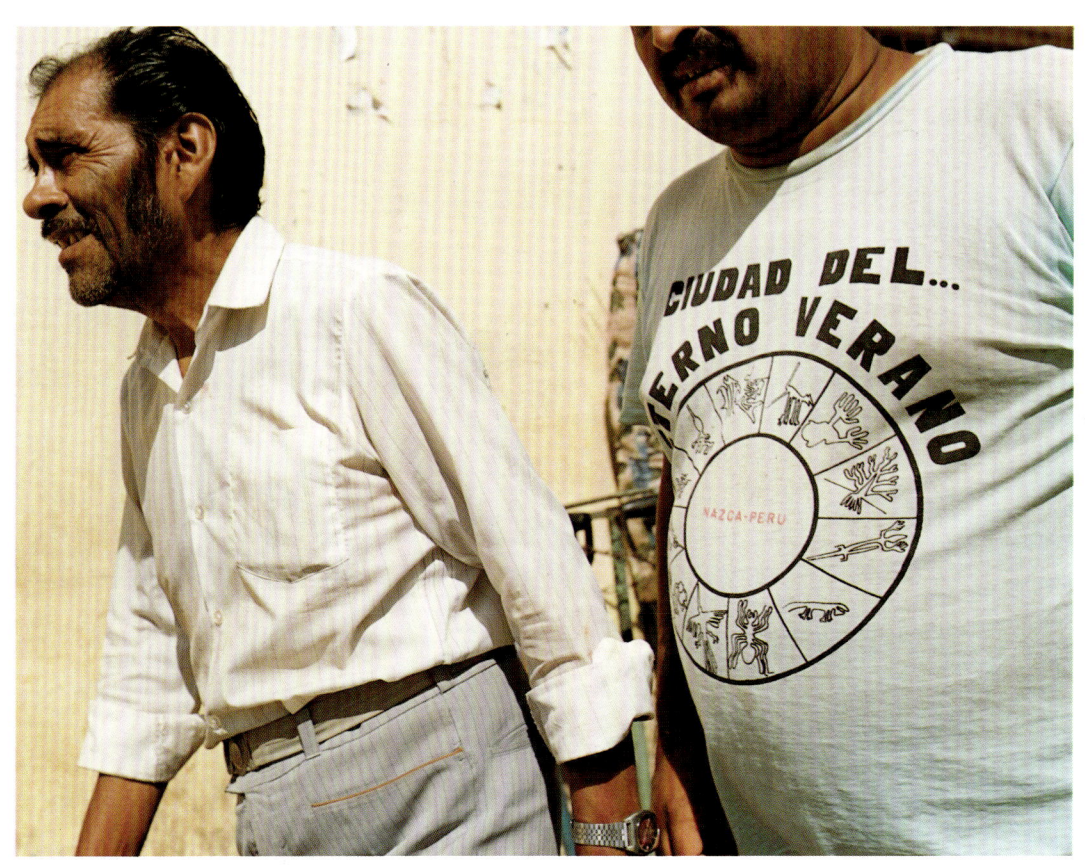

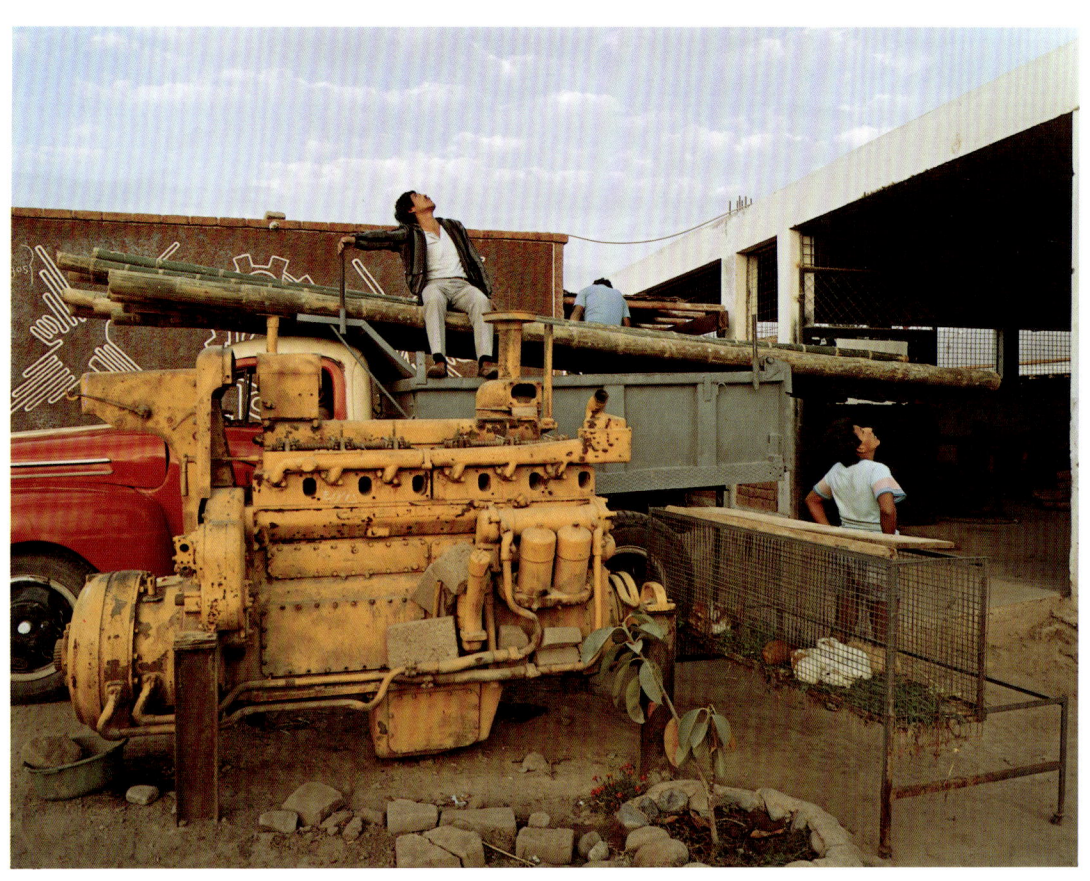

7 • TIMBER YARD

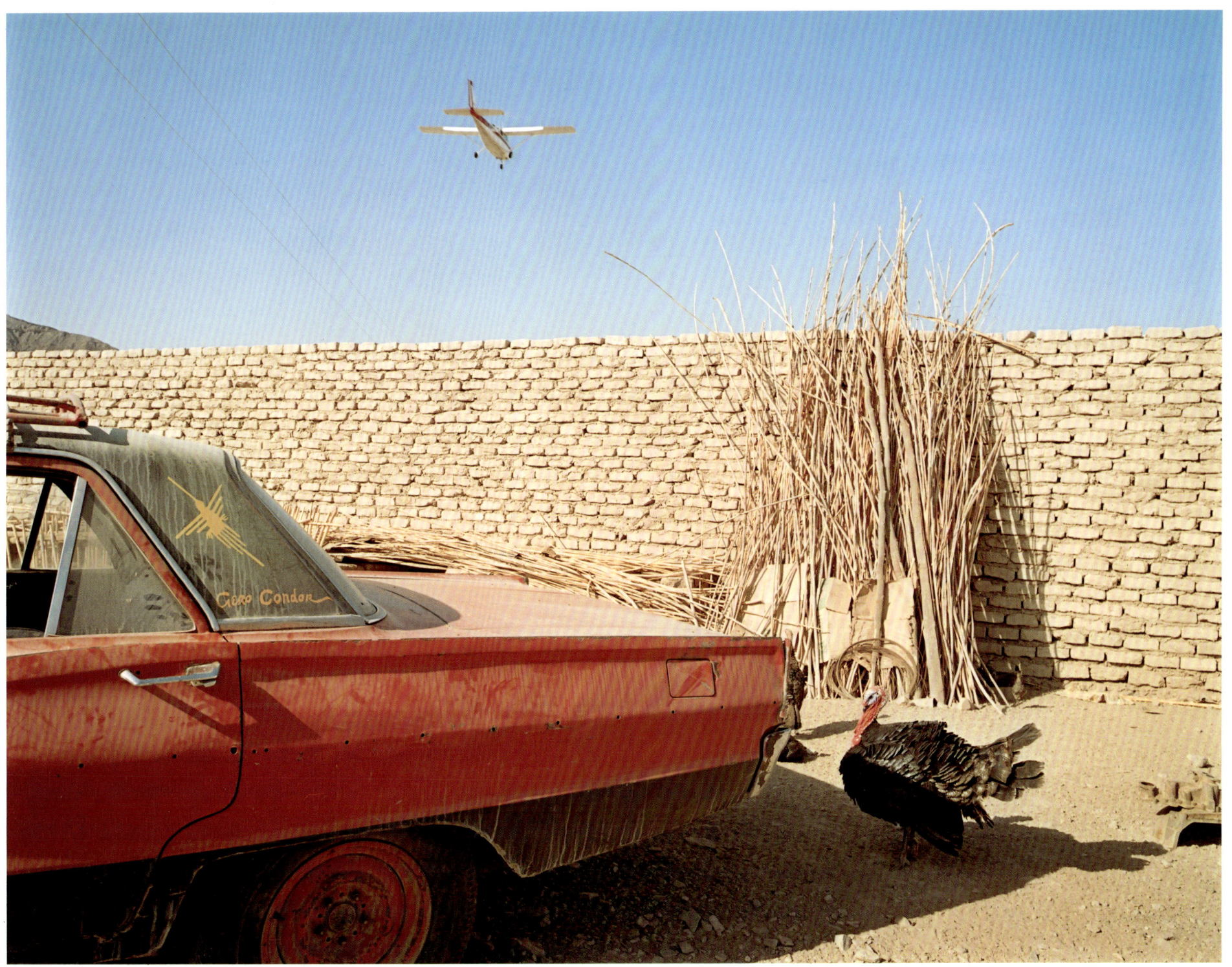

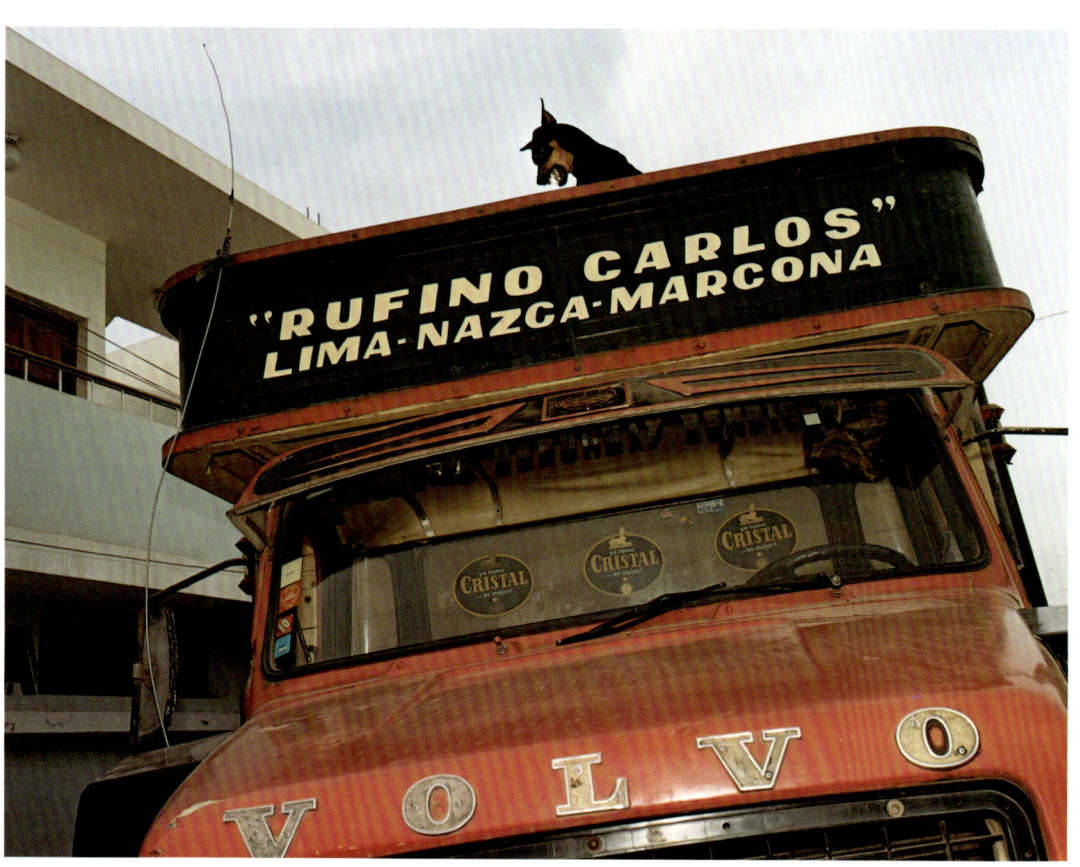

9 • BEER TRUCK

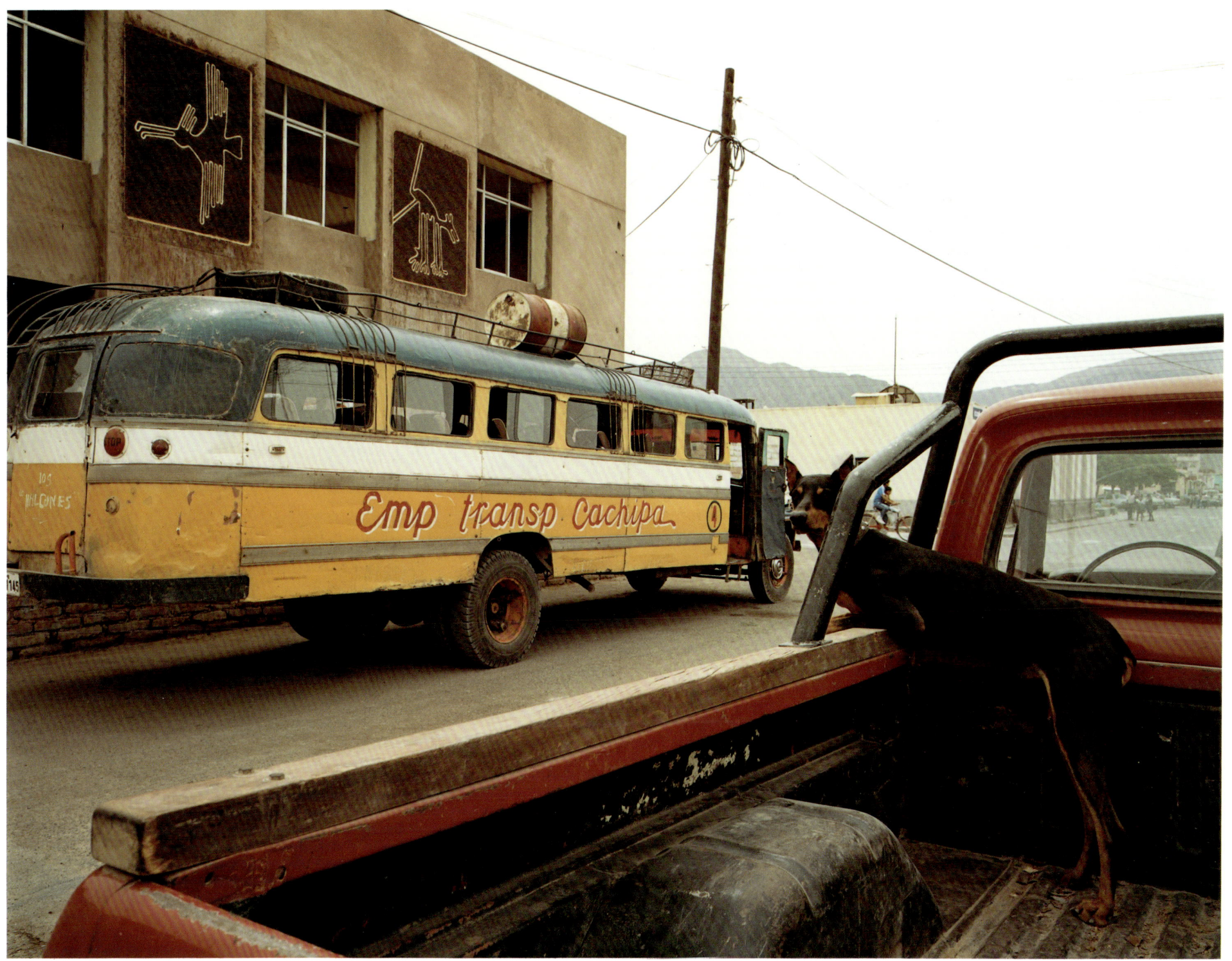

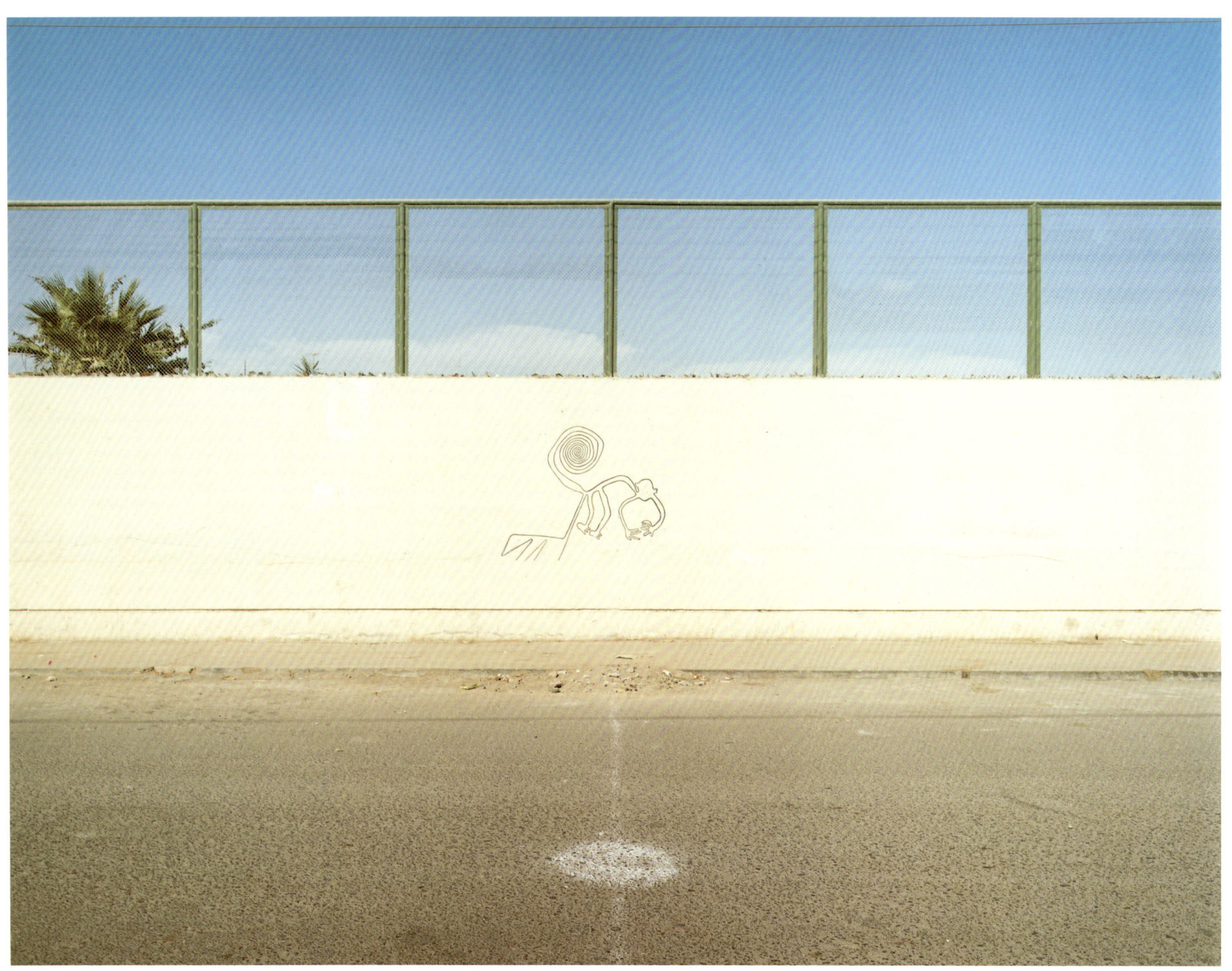

11 • HOTEL WALL & CHALKED FOOTBALL PITCH

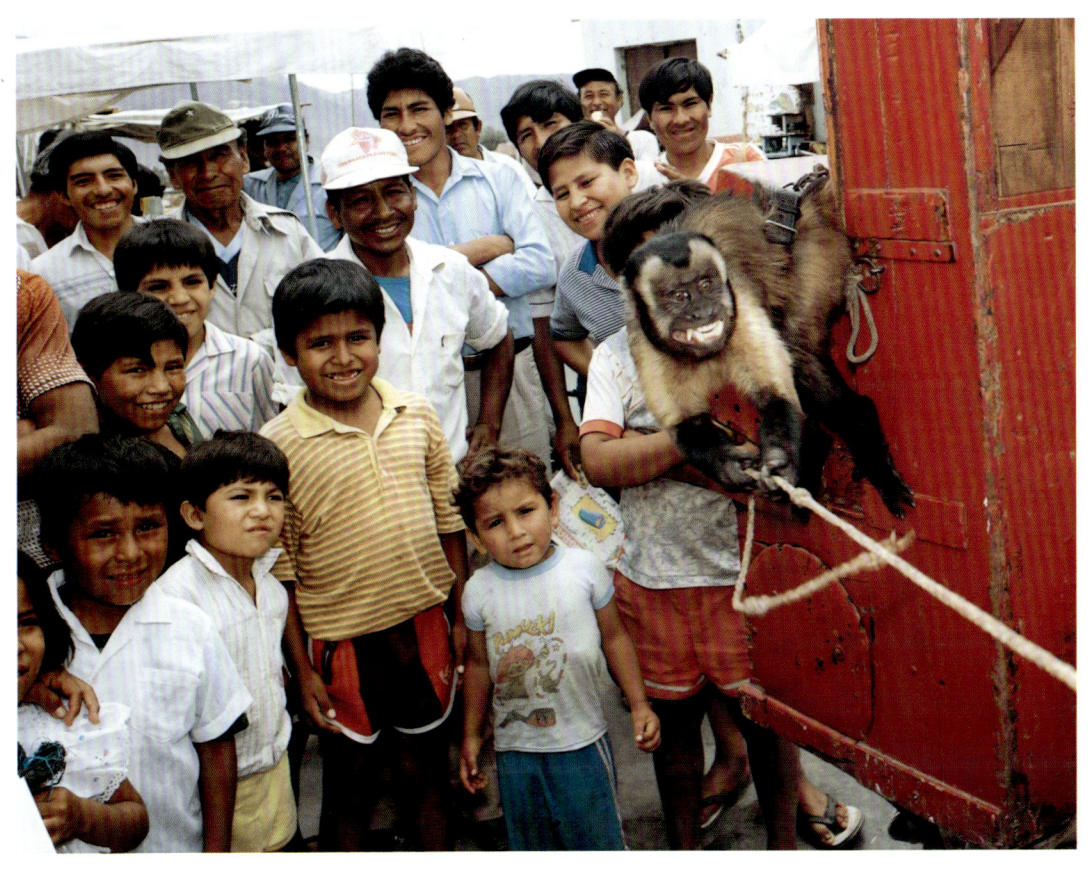

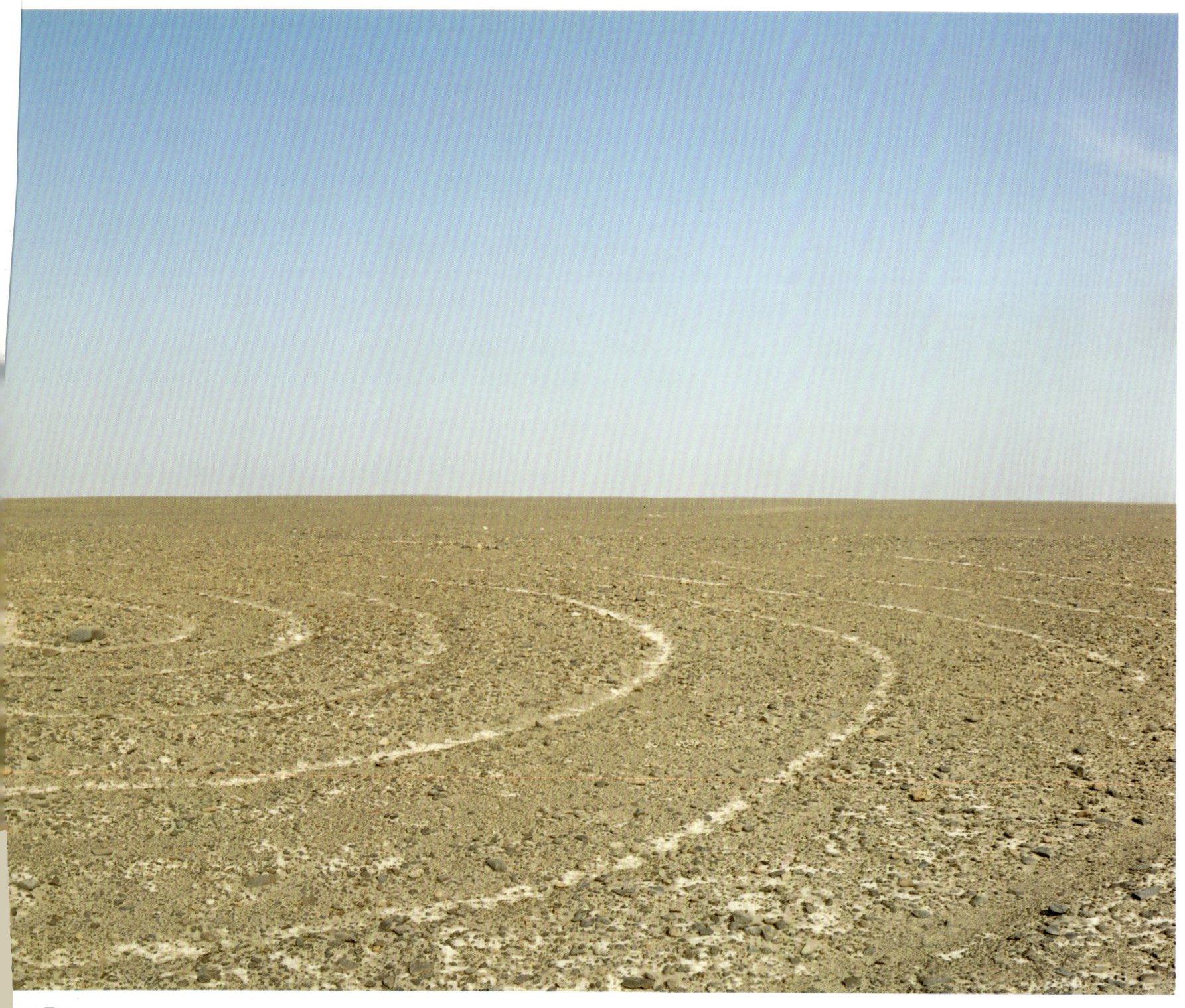

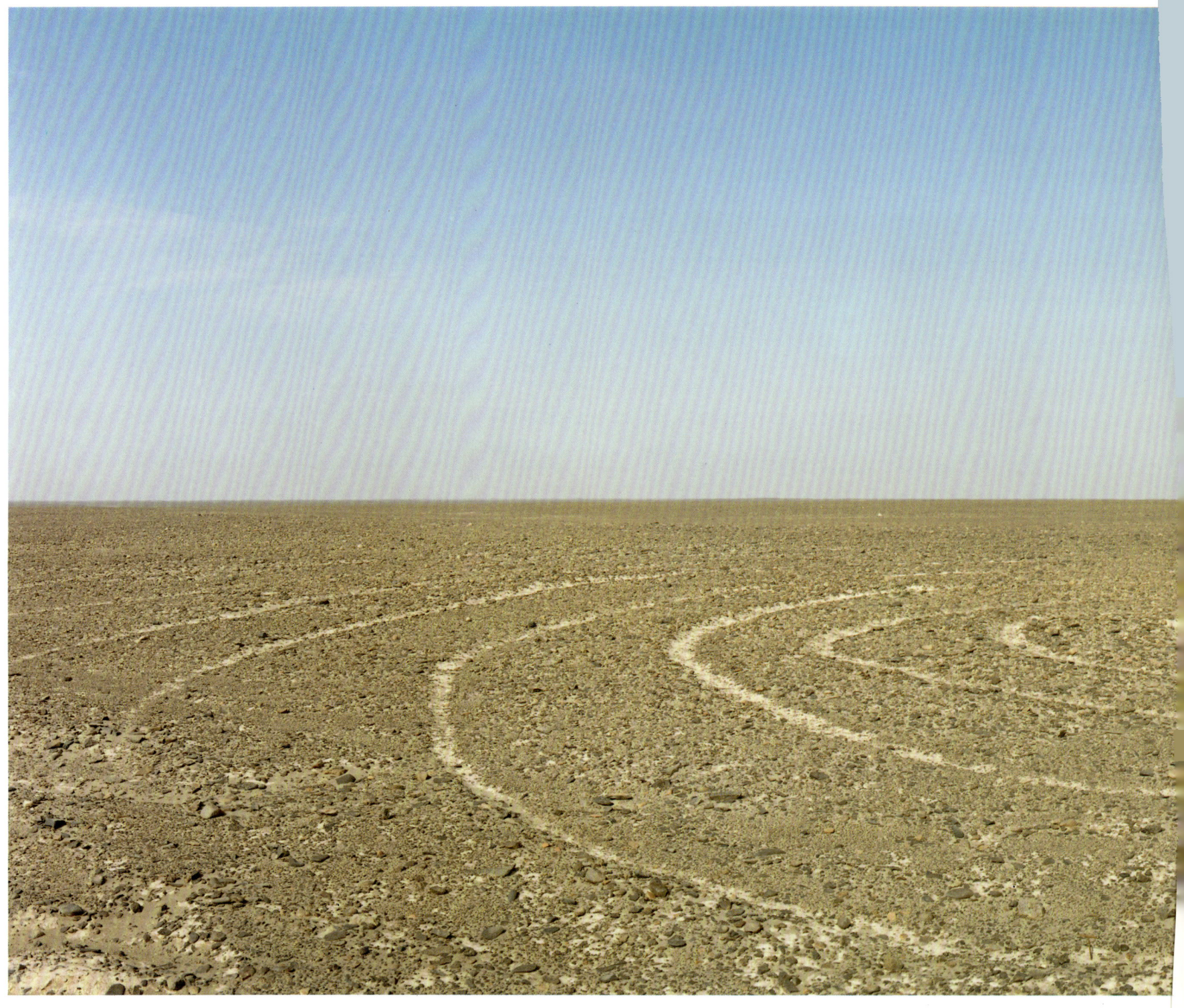

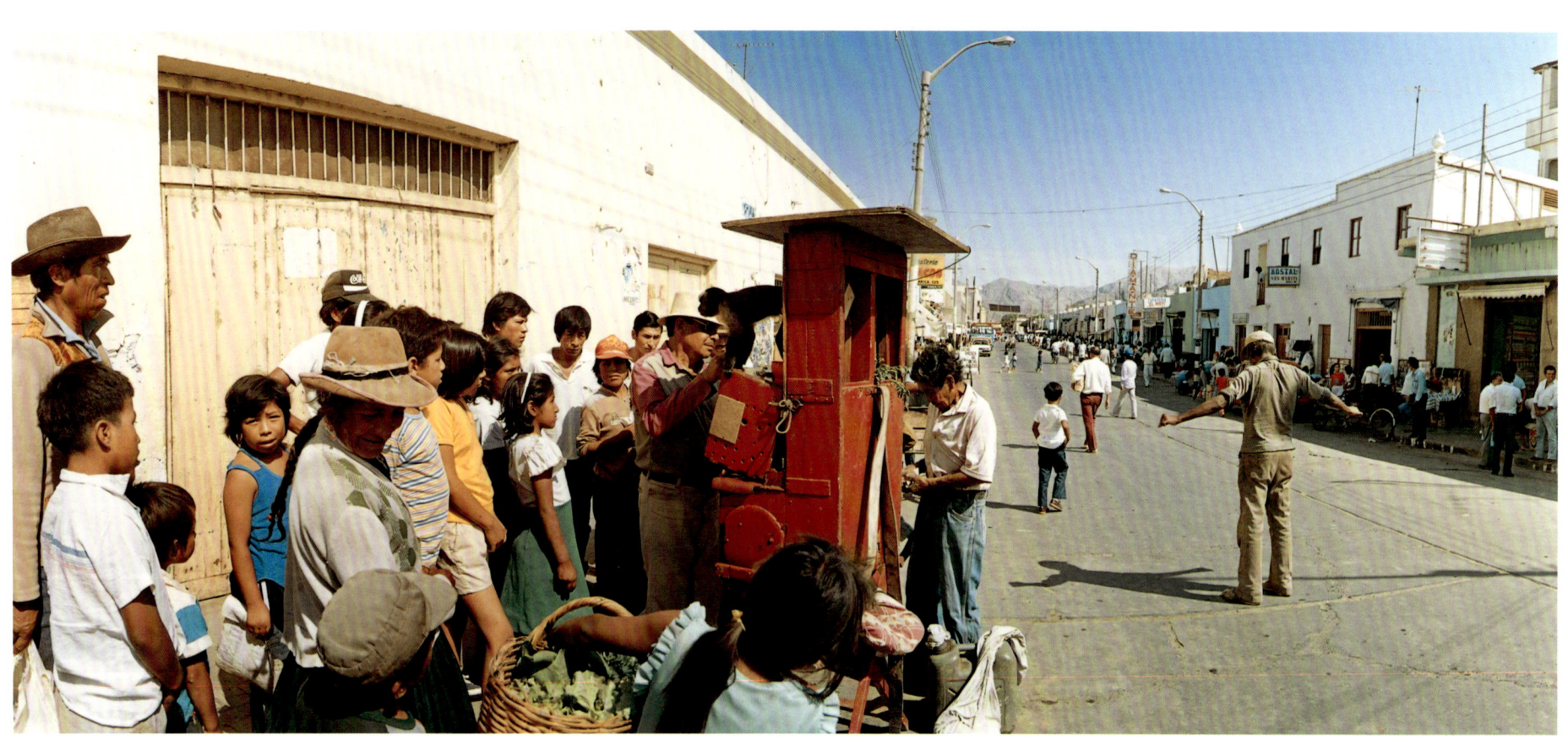

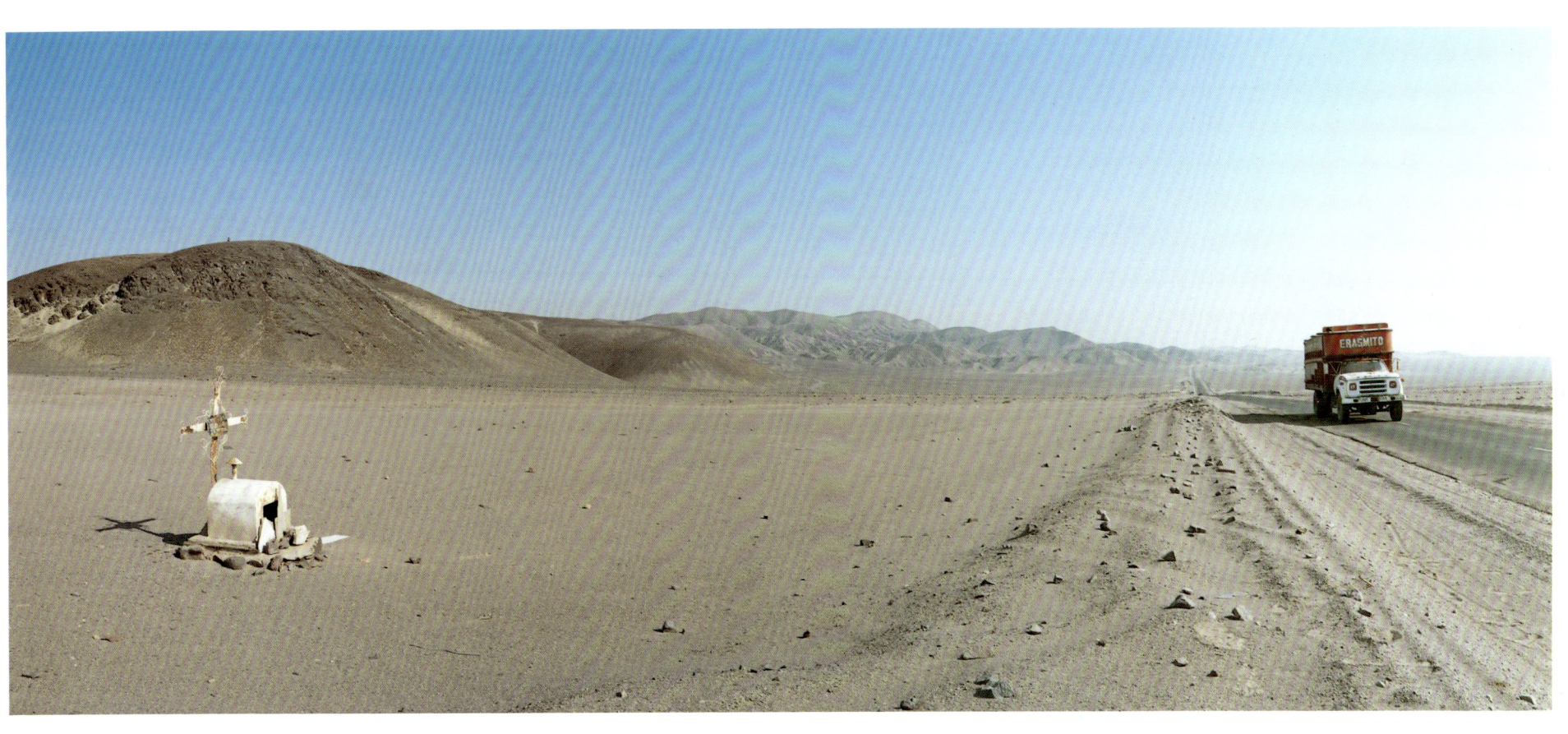

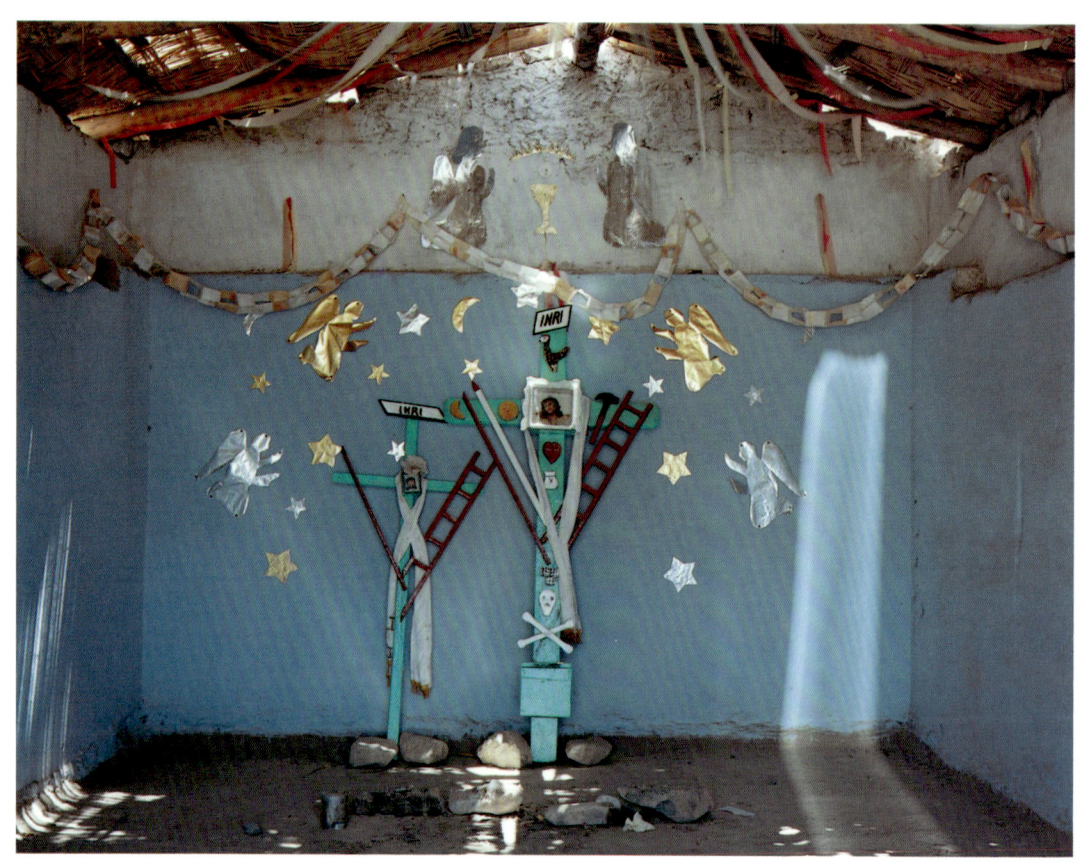

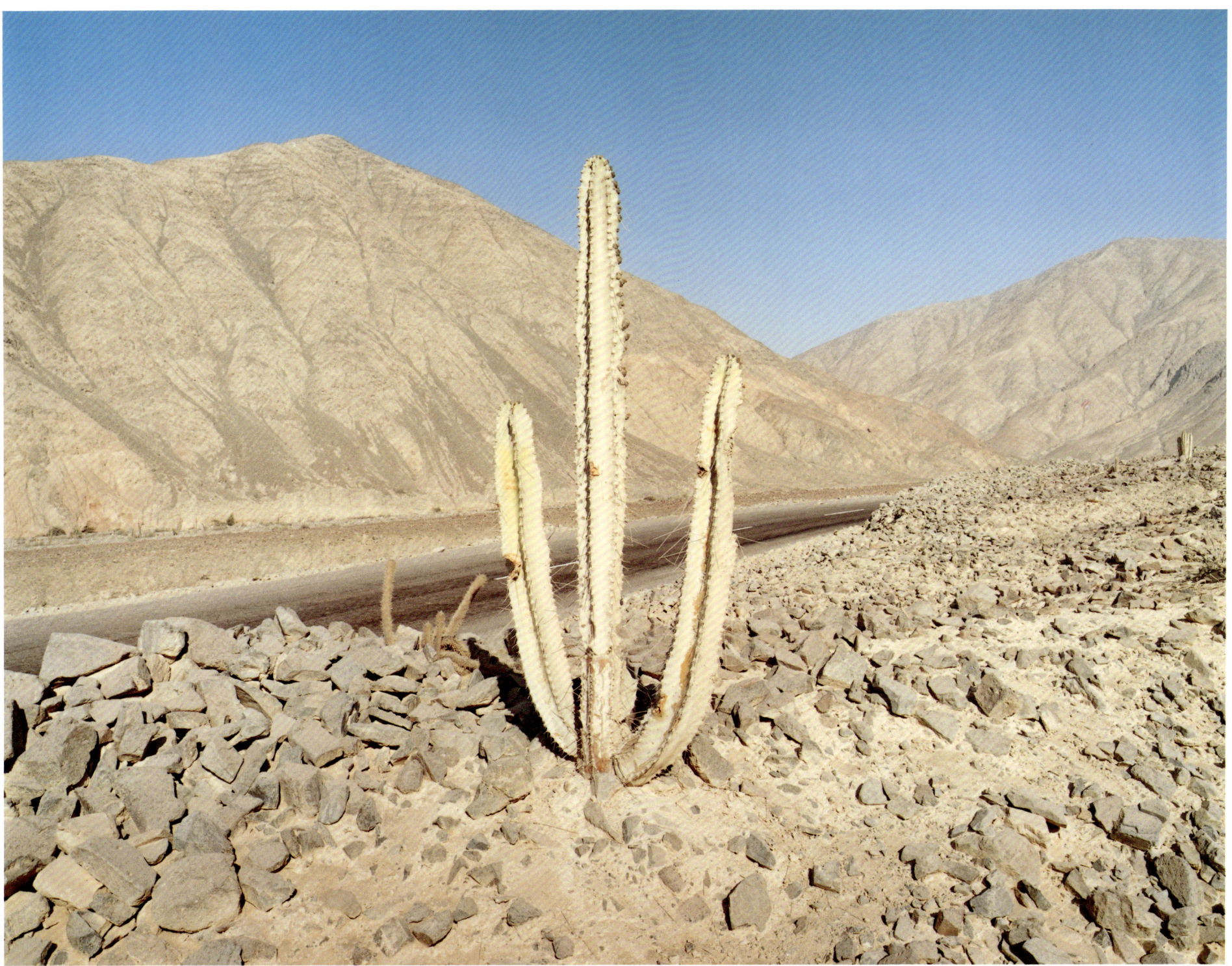

17 • ROAD TO CUZCO

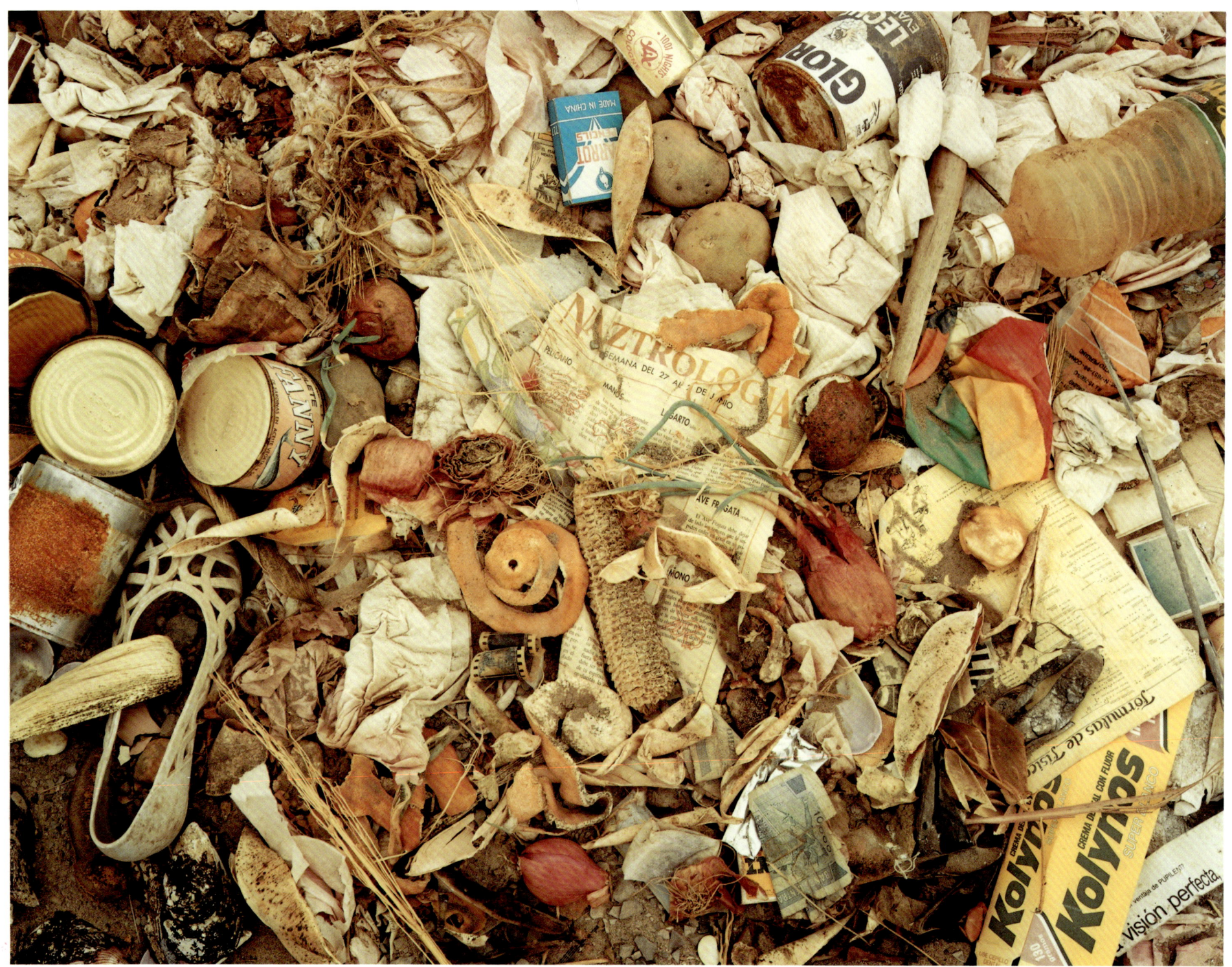

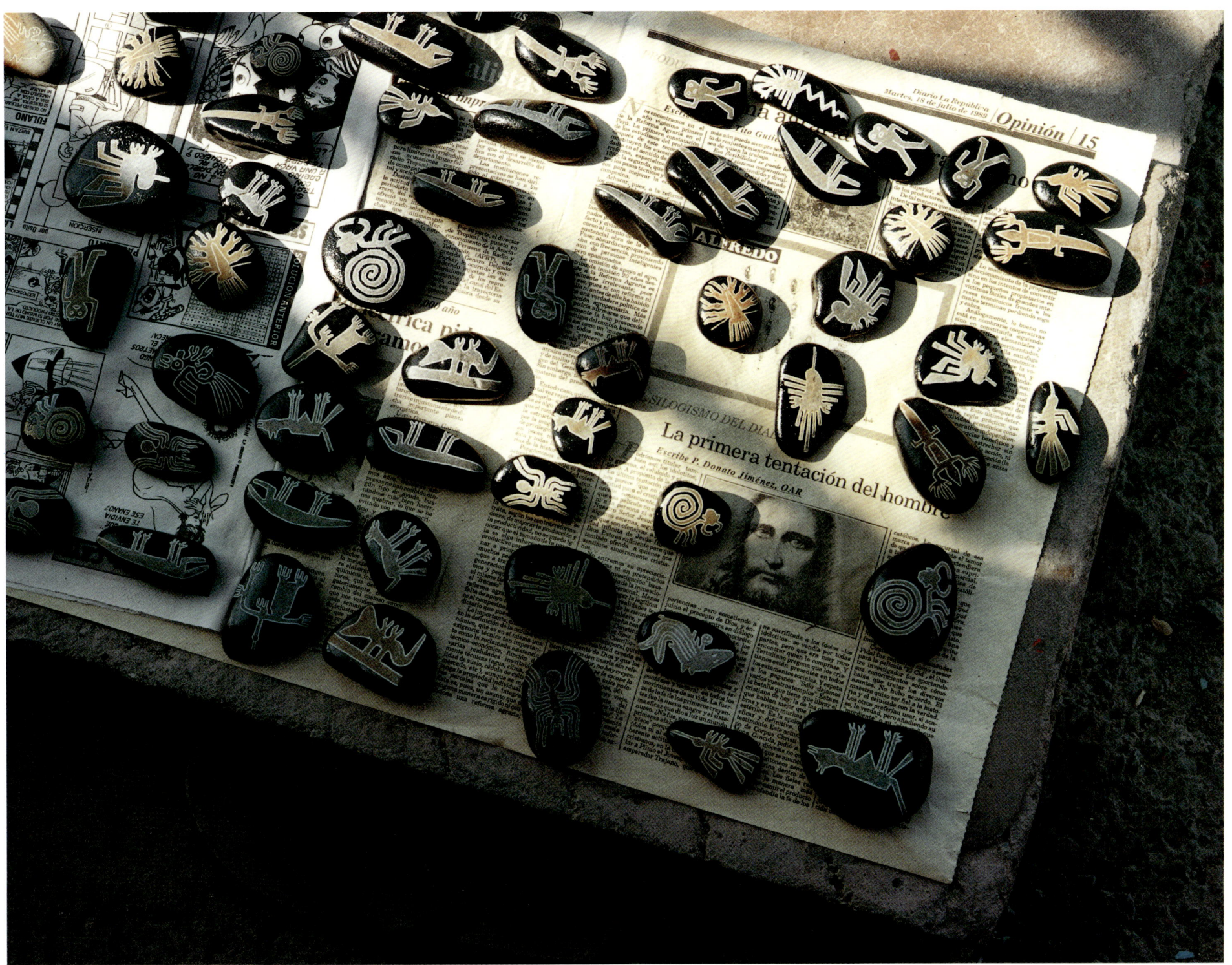

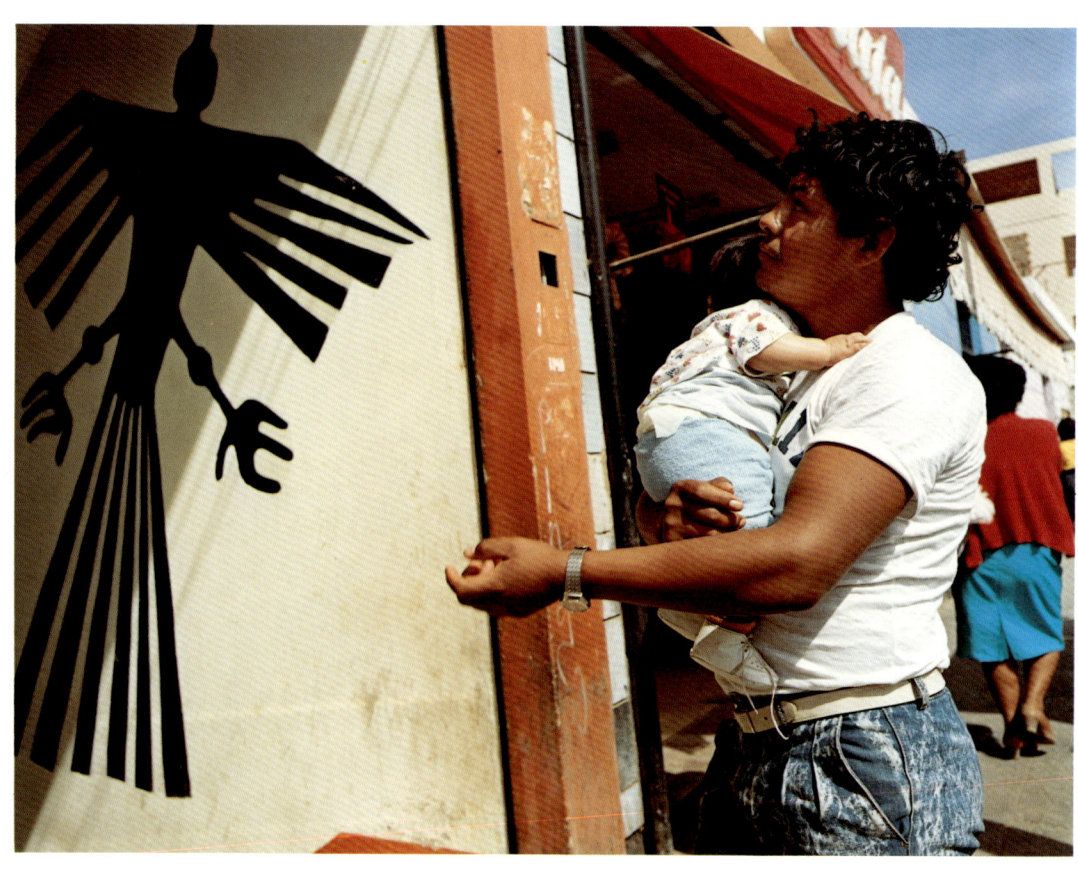

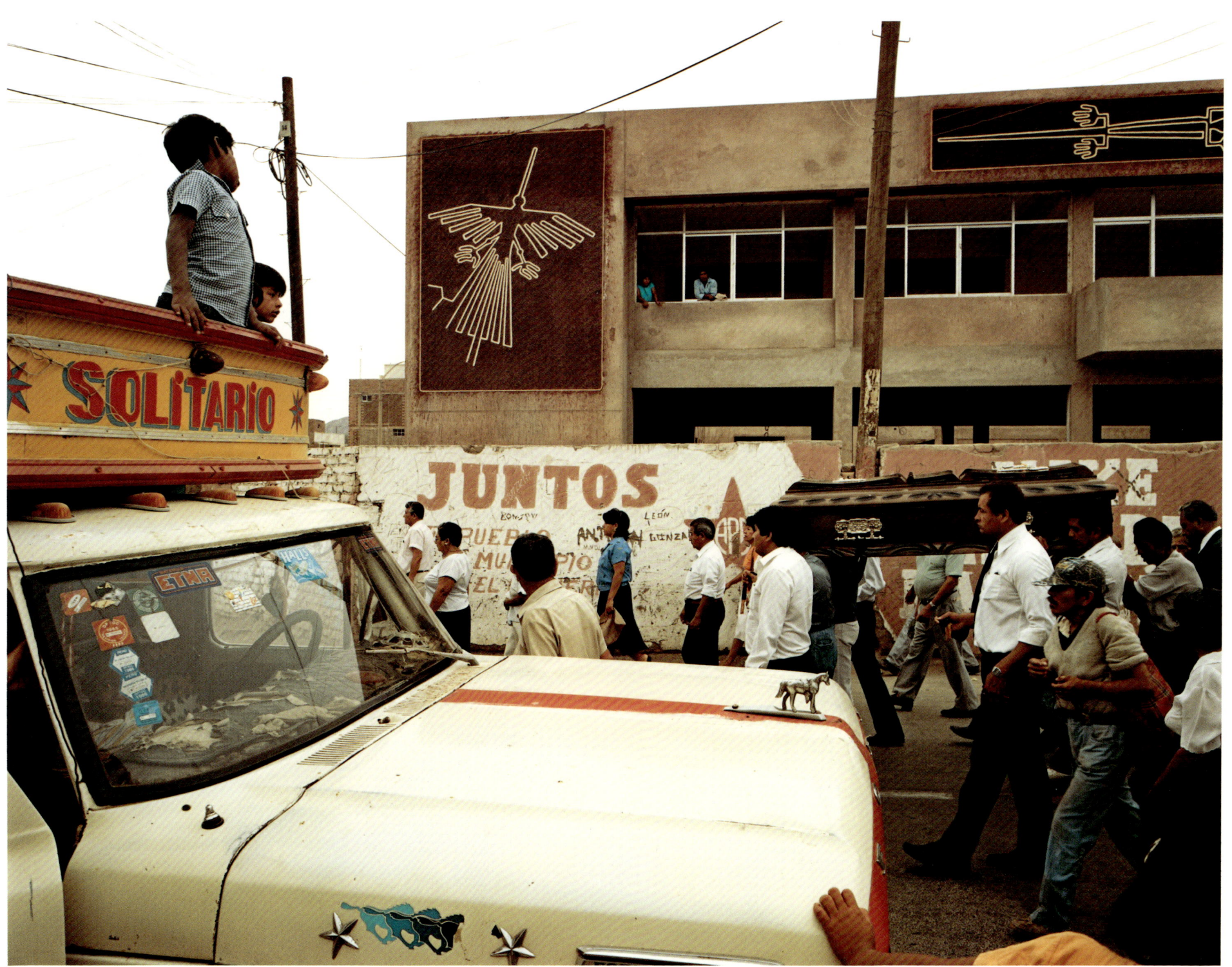

21 • Solitario, Juntos (Alone, Together)

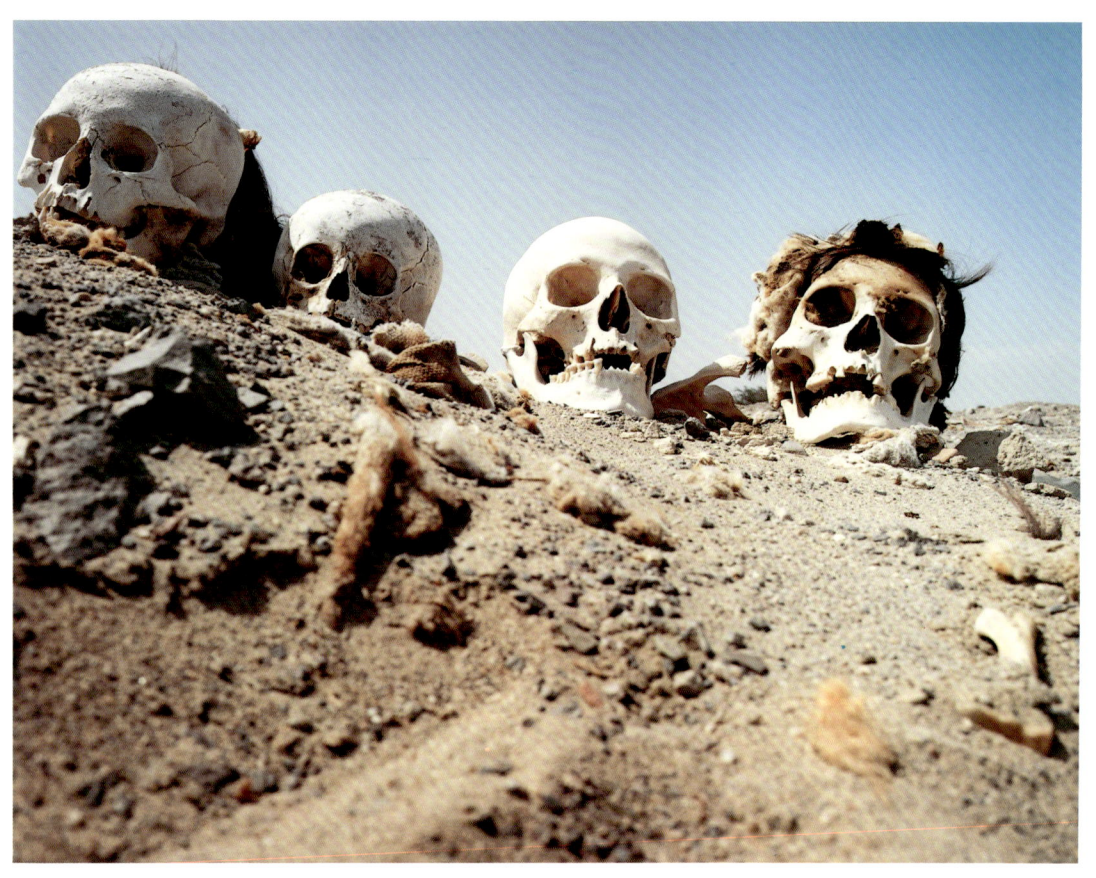

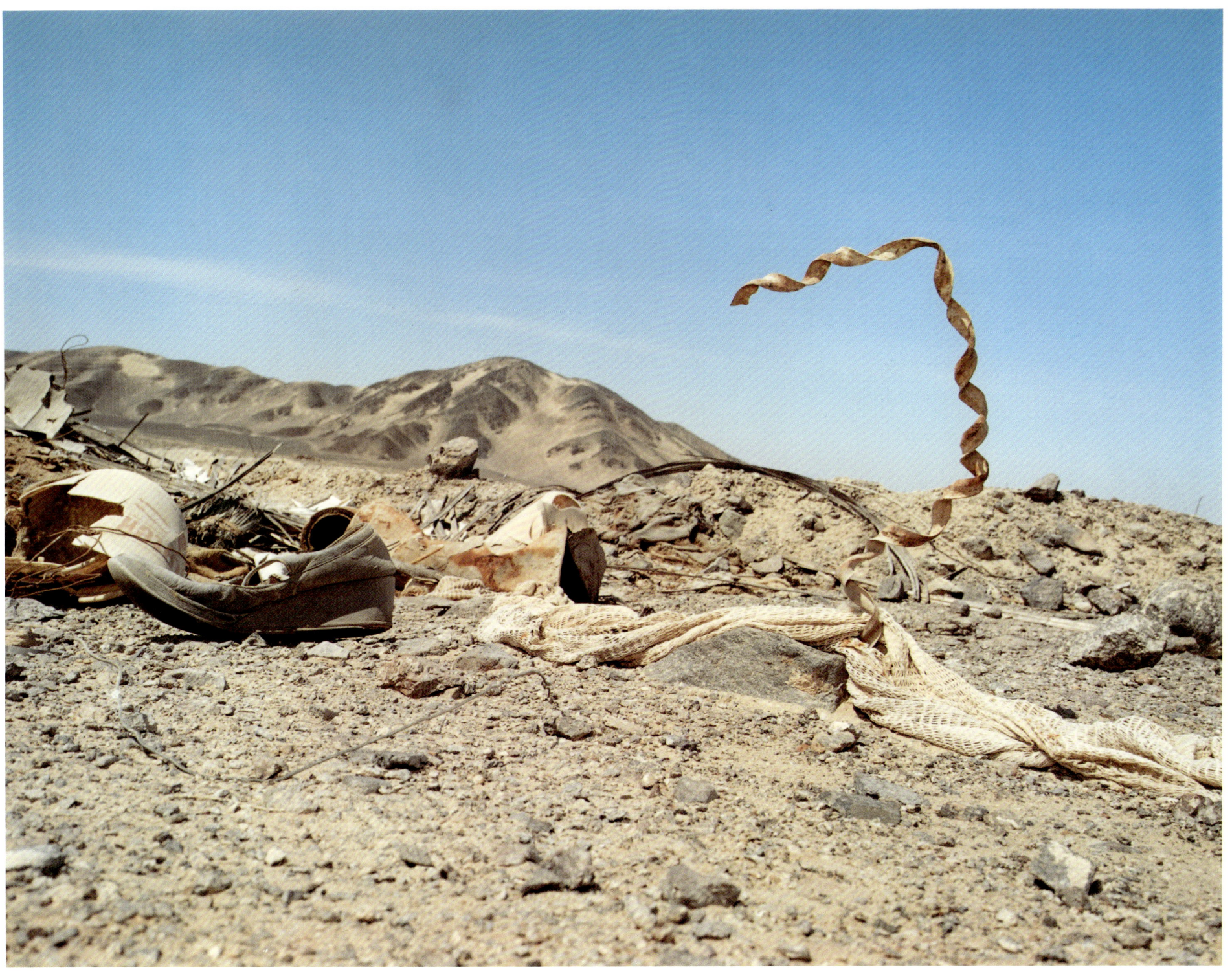

23 • DEBRIS, VISTA ALEGRE

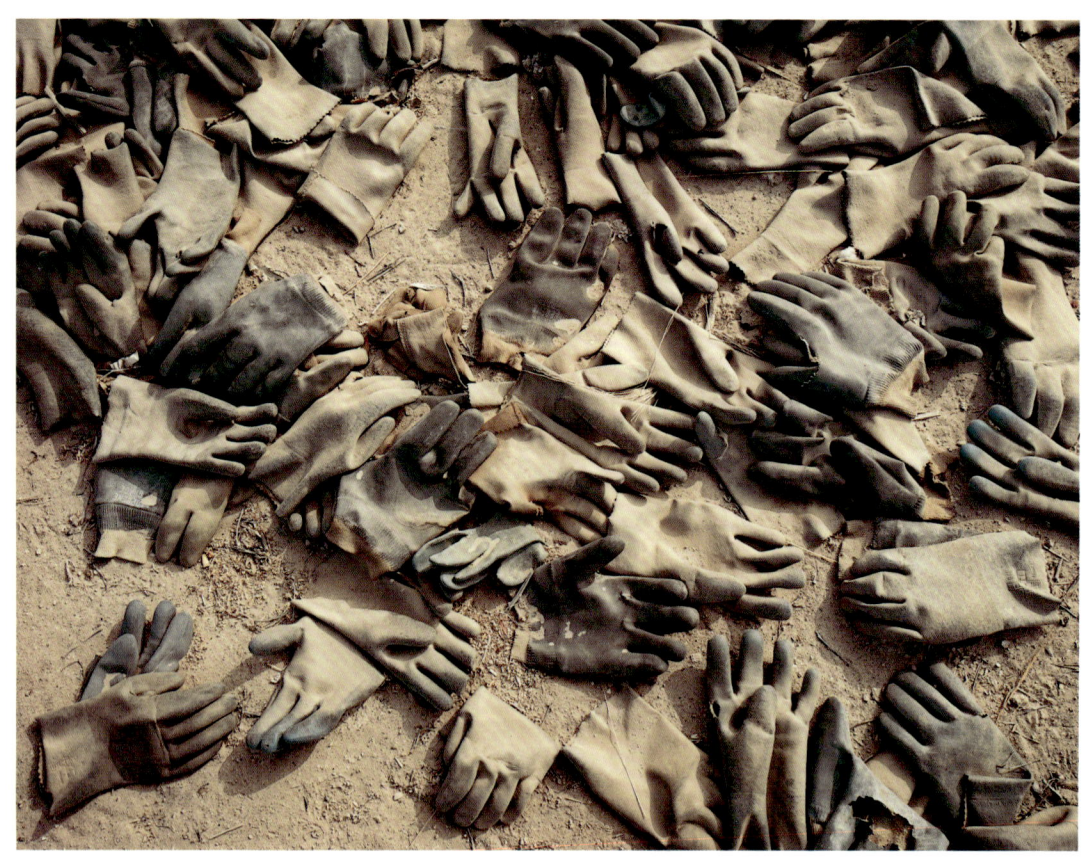

24 • MINERS GLOVES

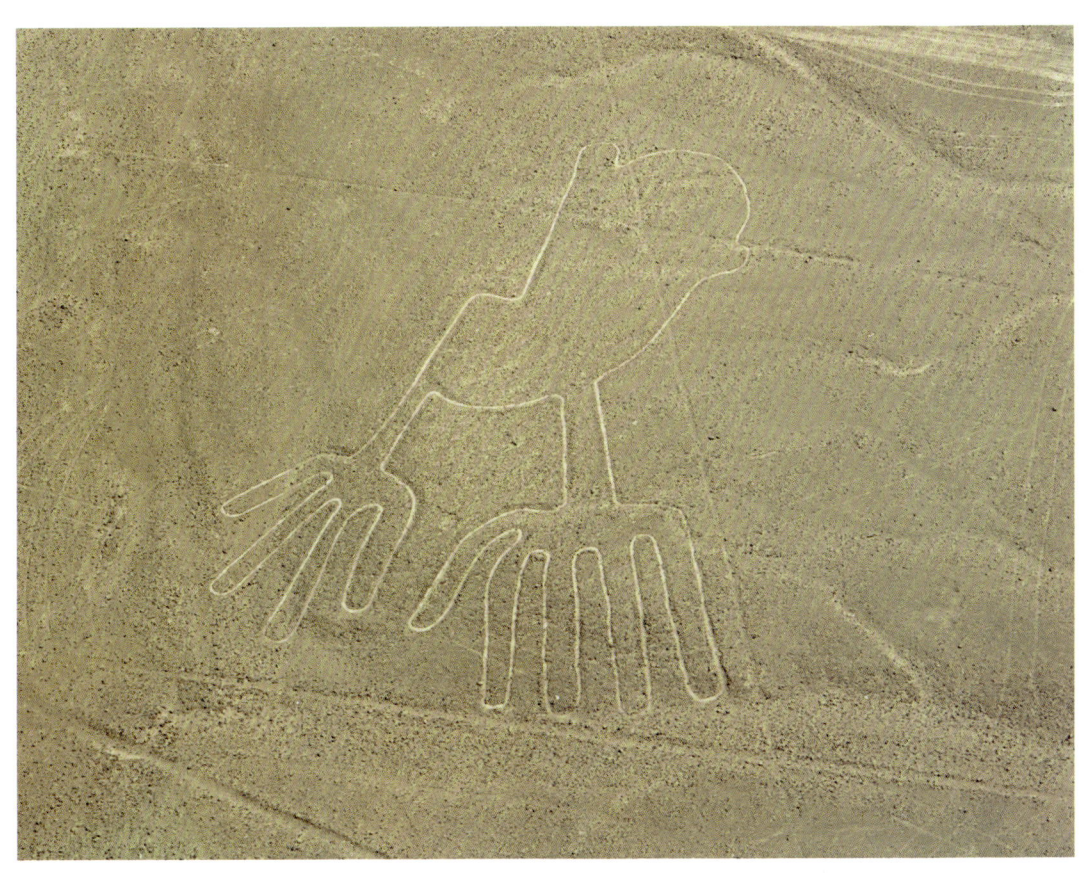

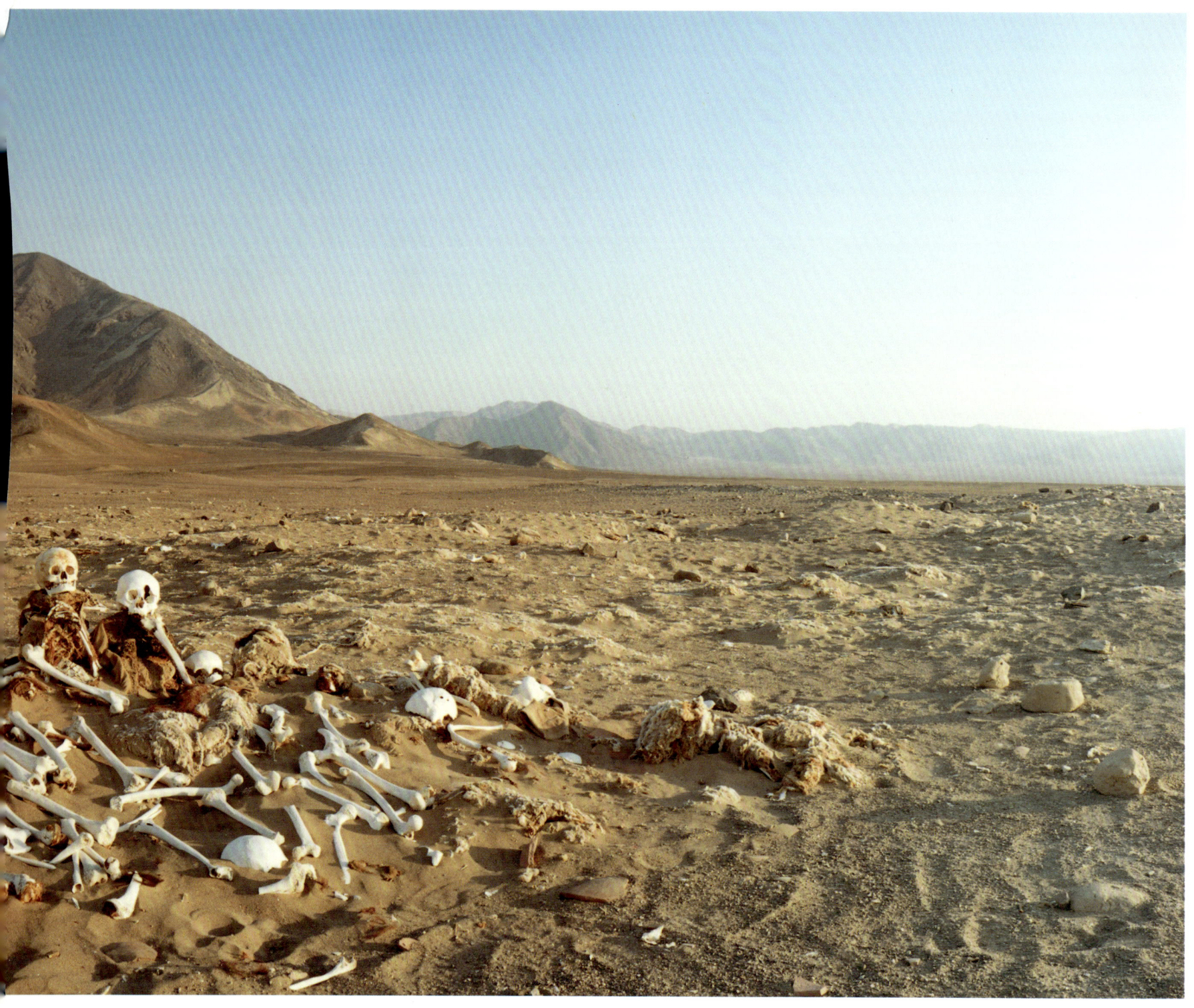

LA CEMETERY

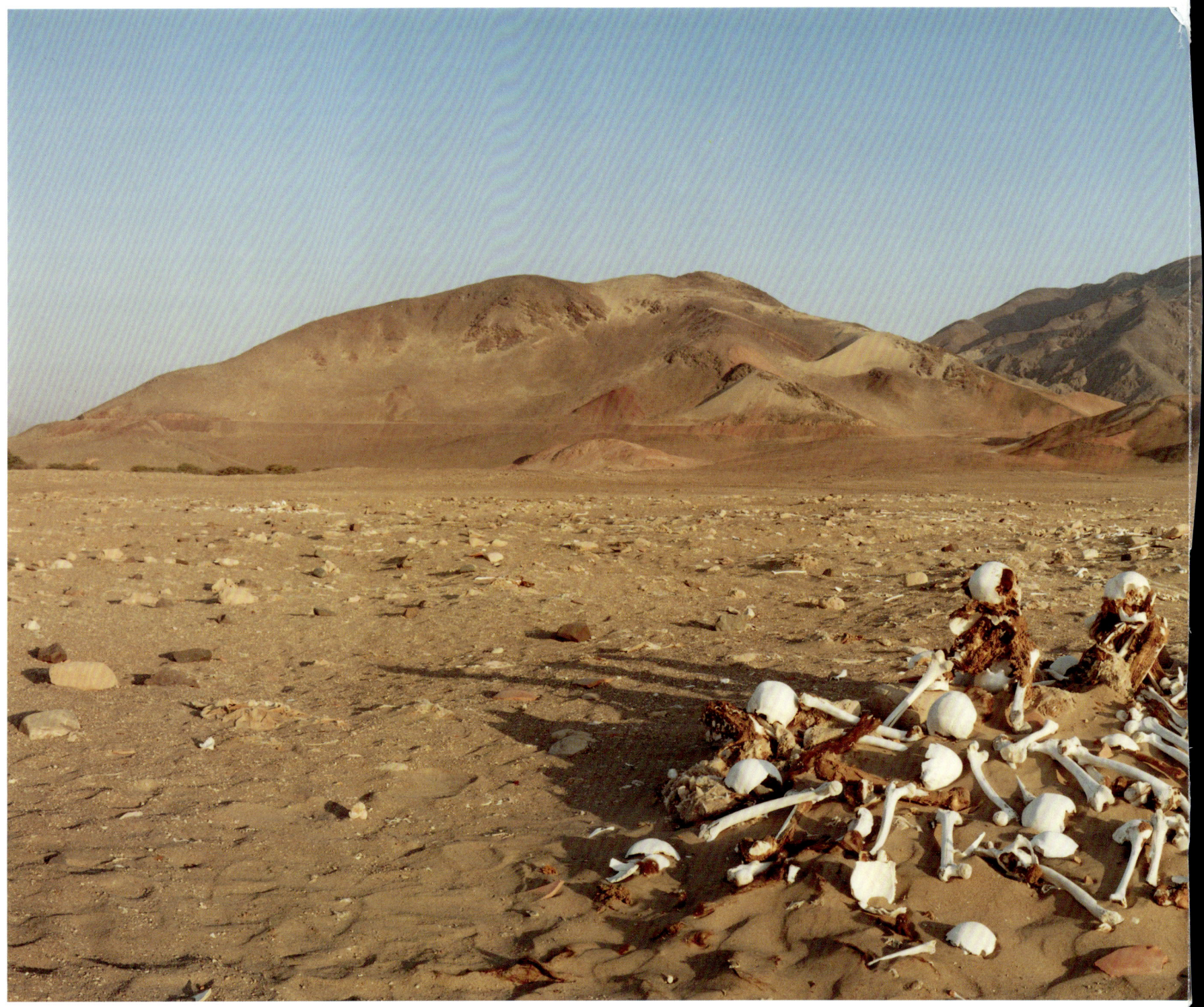

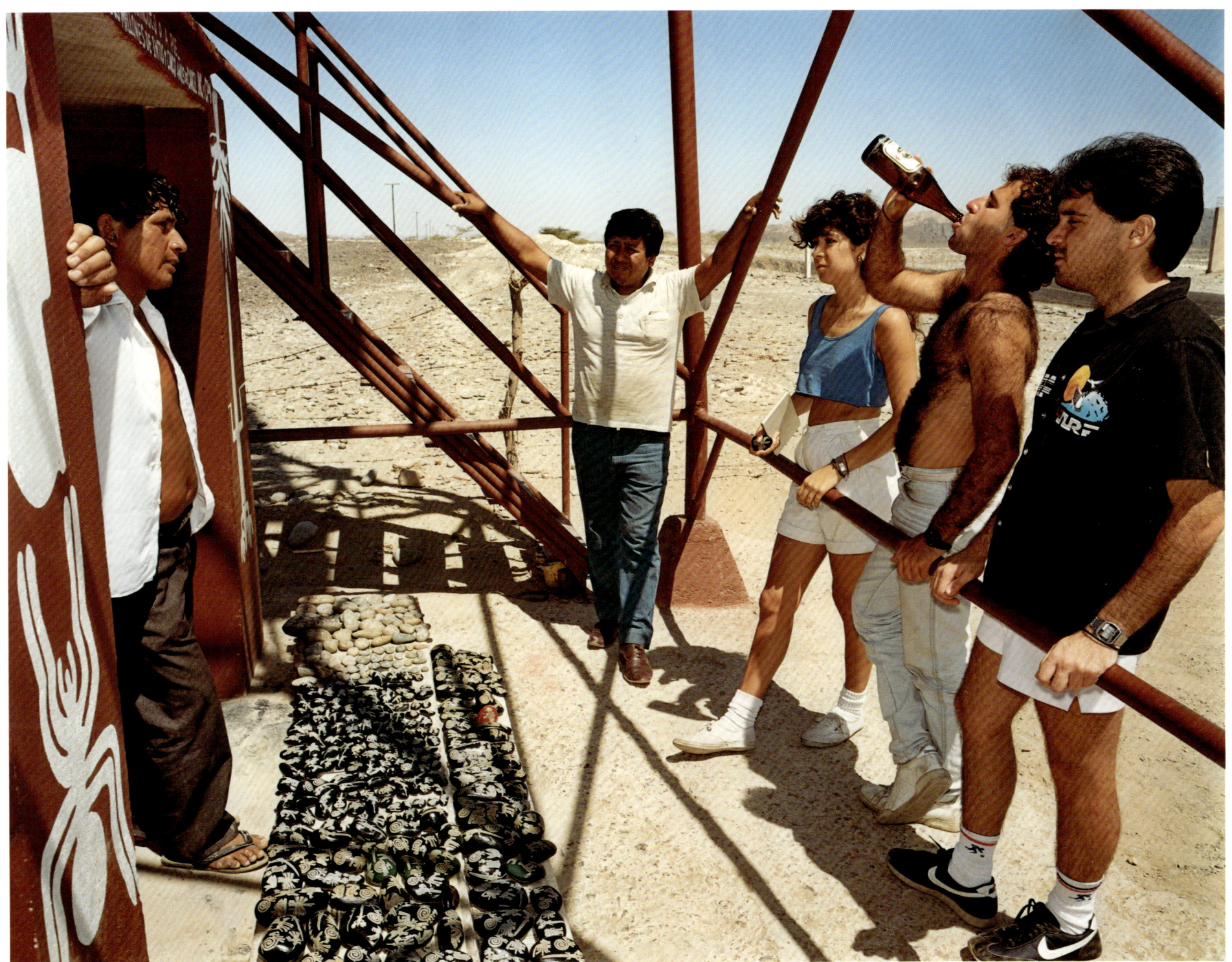

27 • TOURISTS FROM LIMA

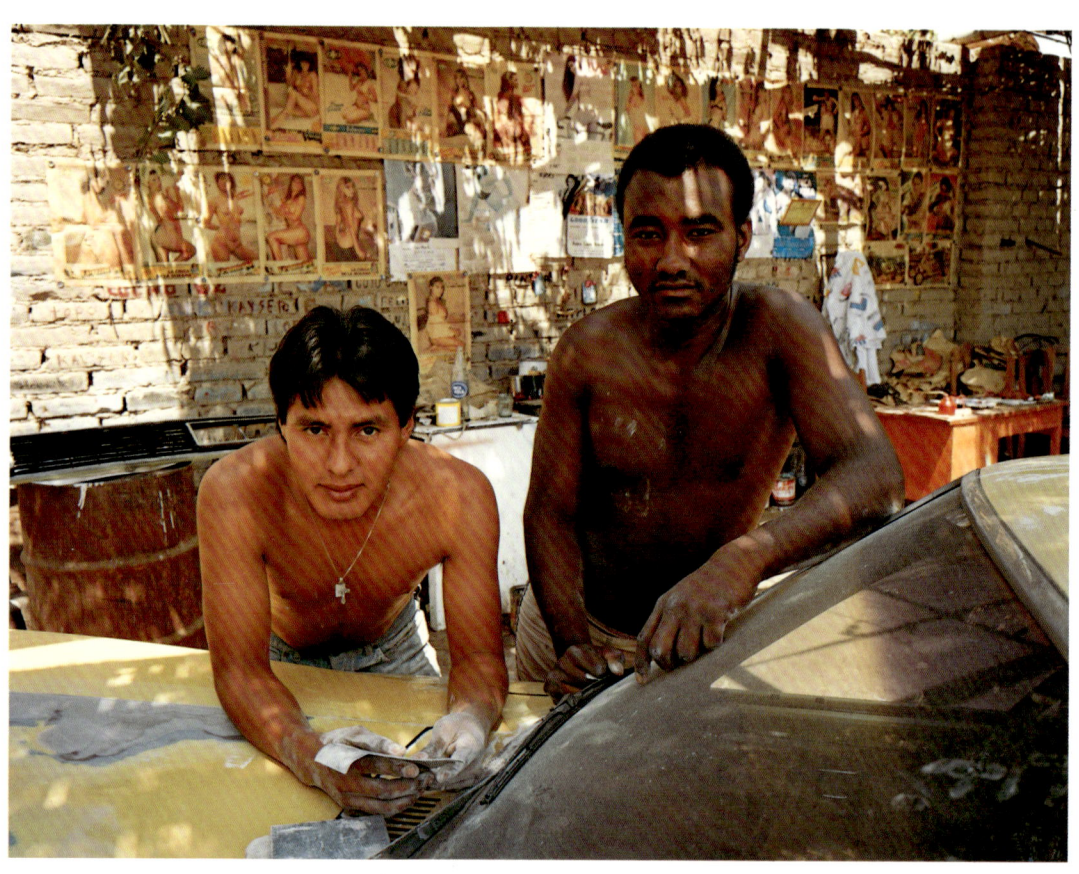

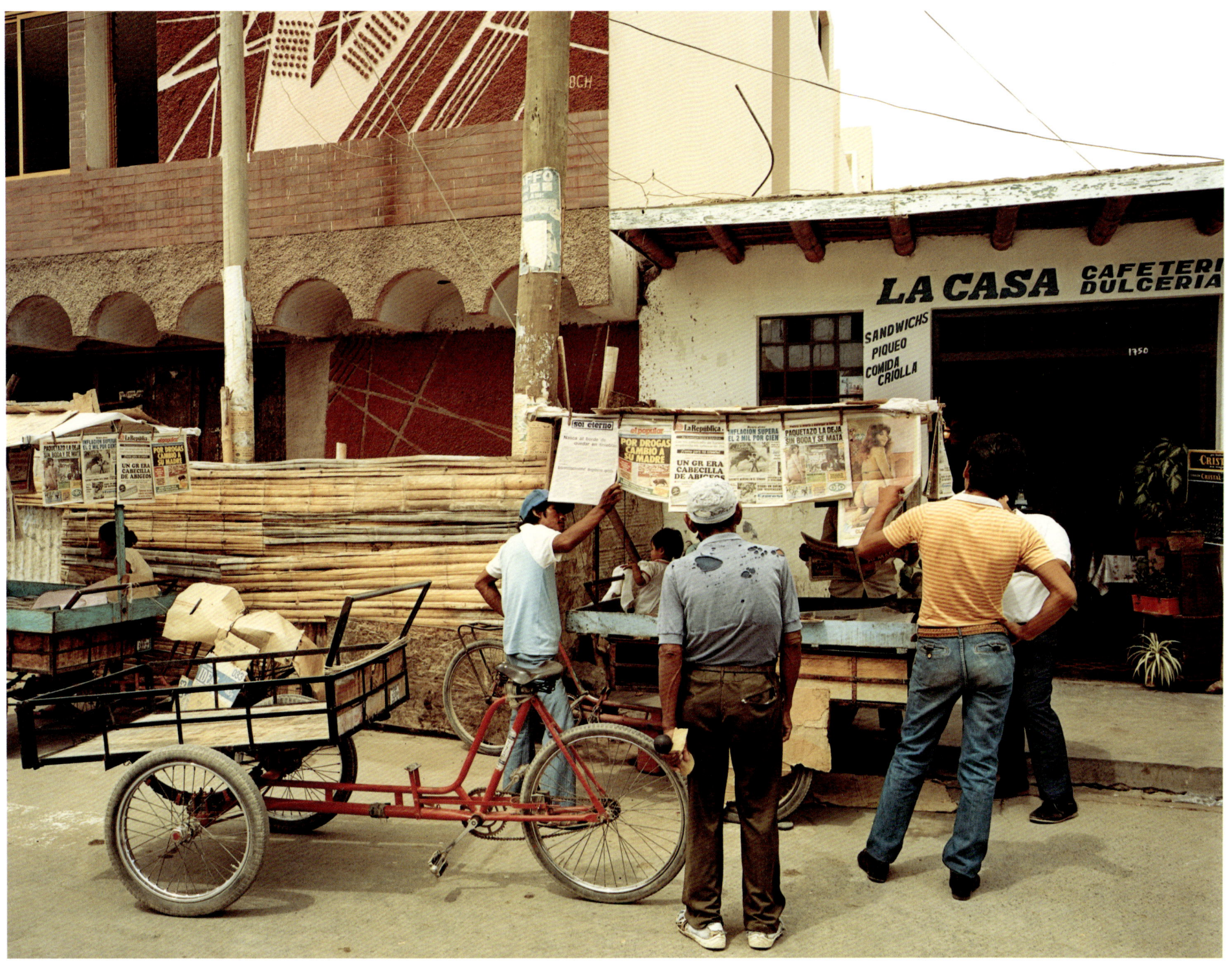

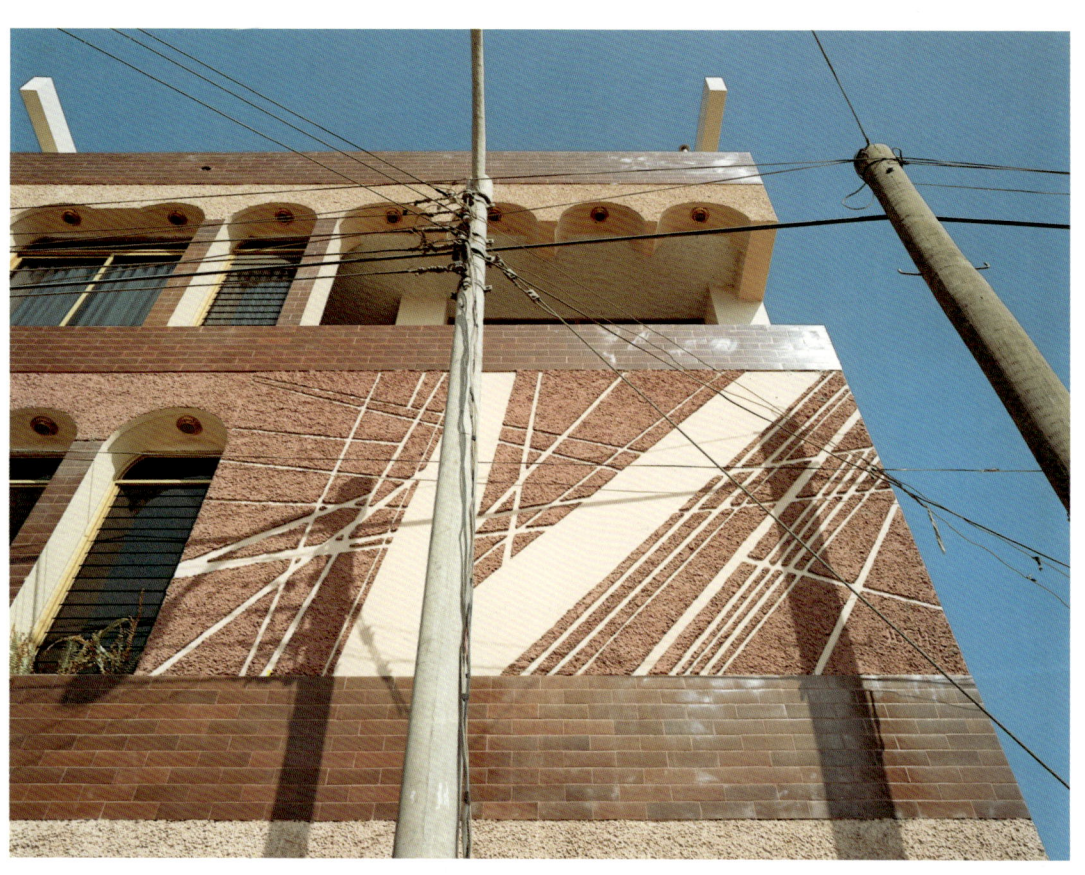

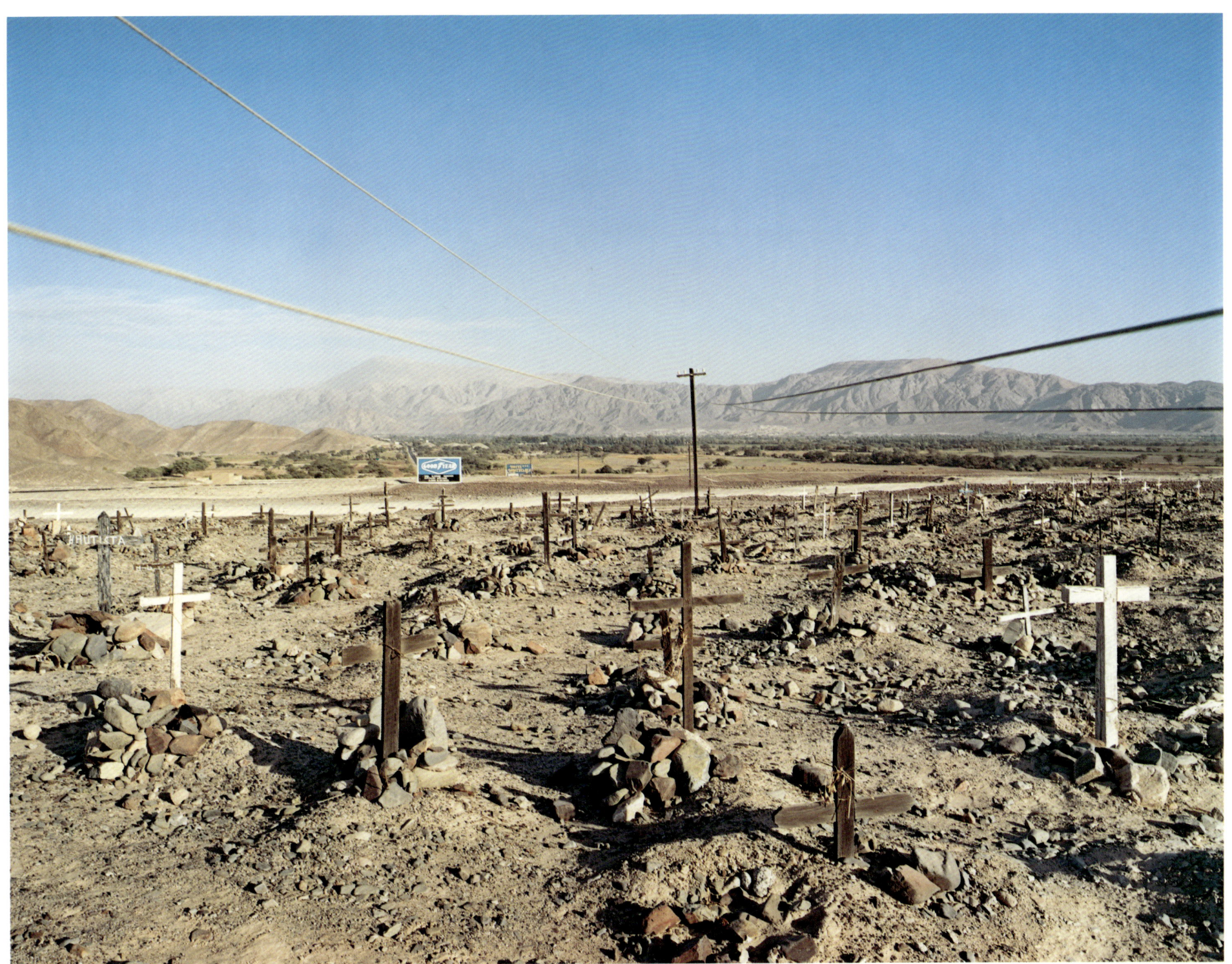

31 • PANAMERICAN HIGHWAY APPROACHING NAZCA

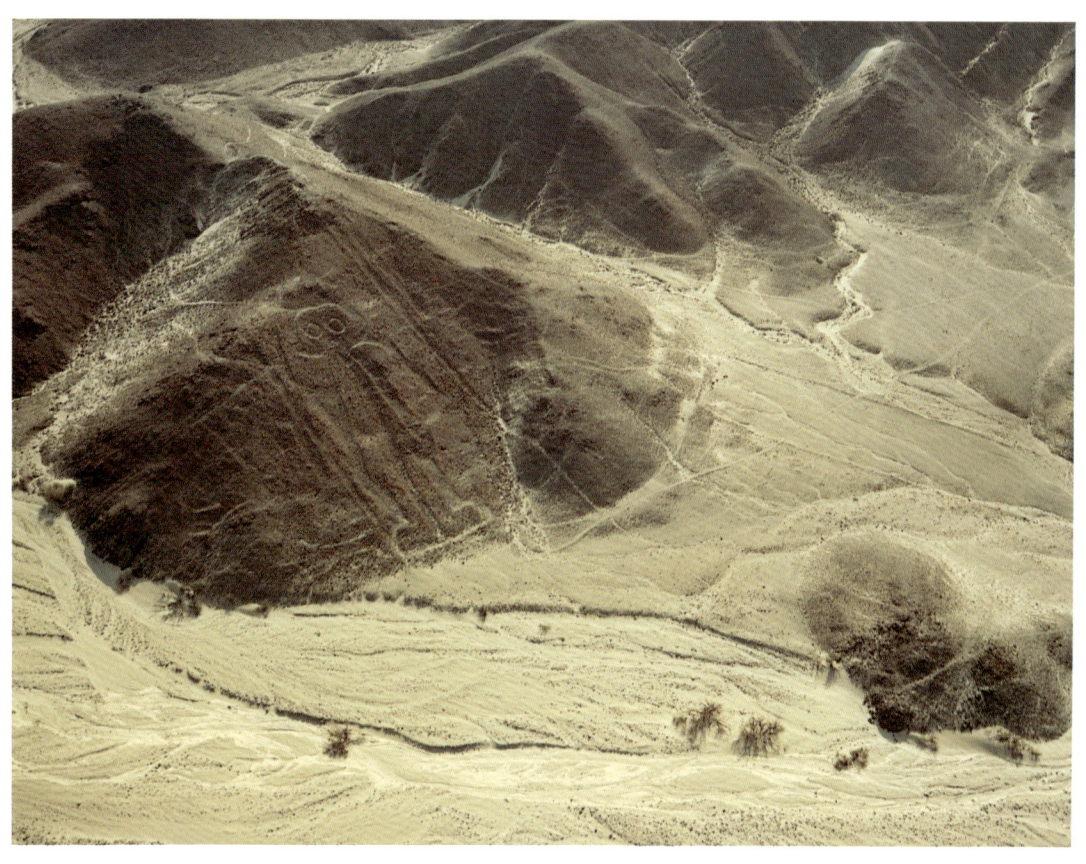

32 • 'OWLMAN' (ASTRONAUT)

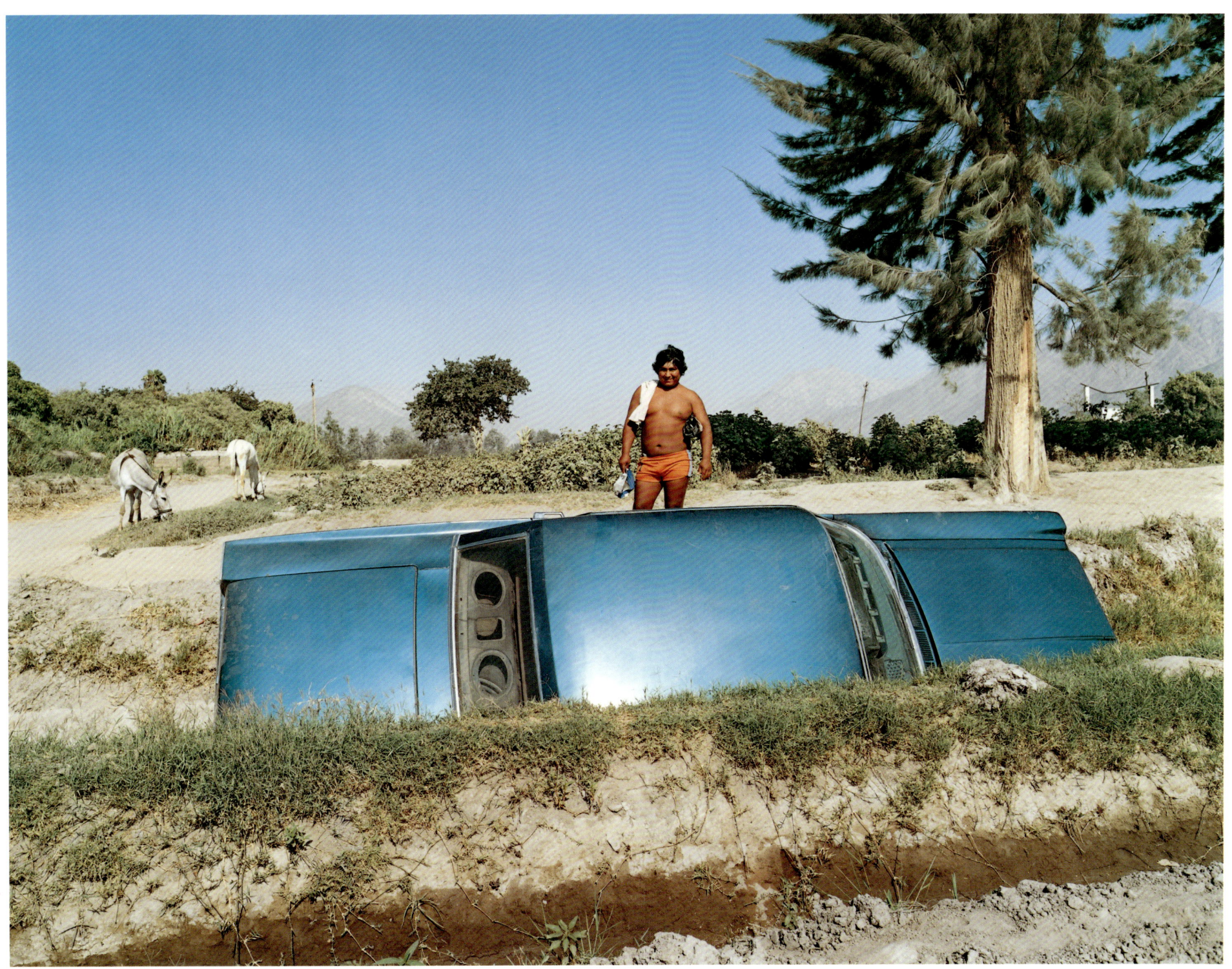

33 • IRRIGATION DITCH WITH TAXI

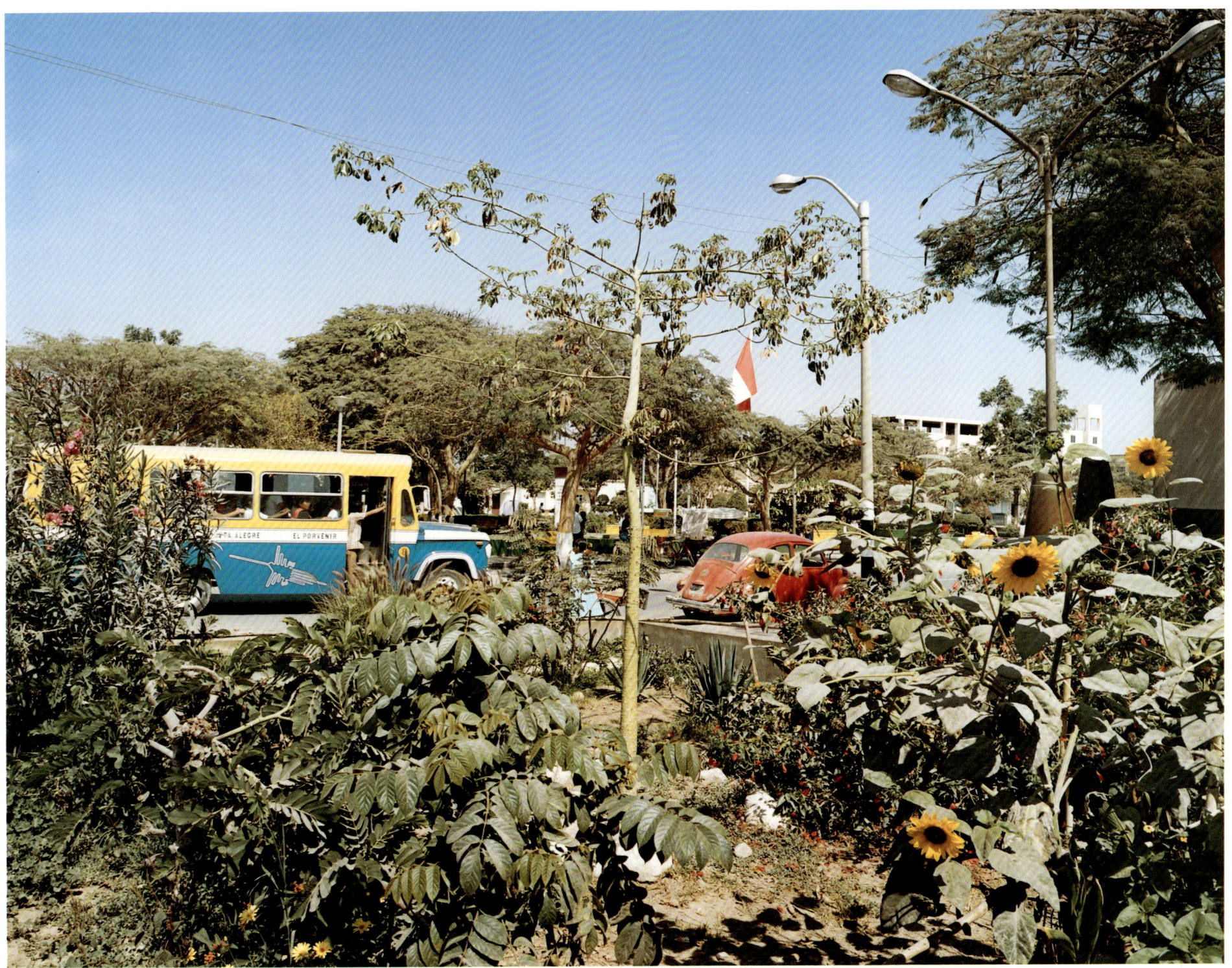

34 • Plaza de Armas, Nazca

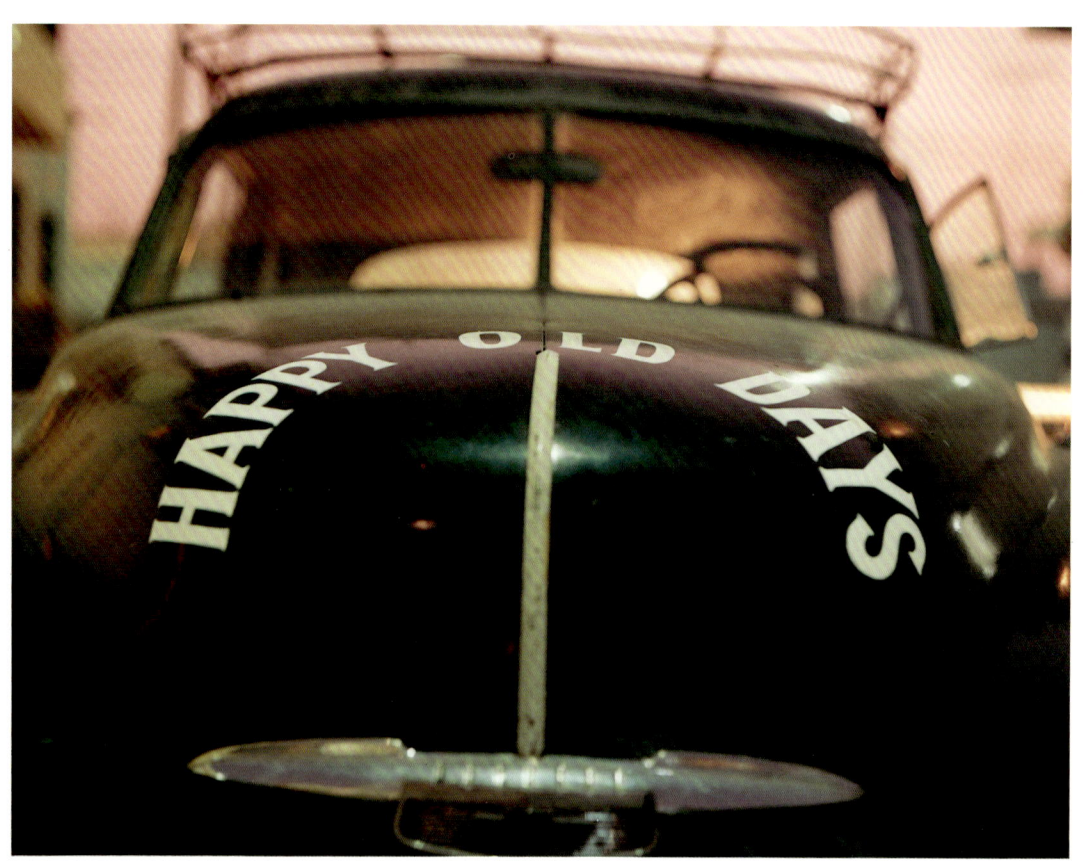

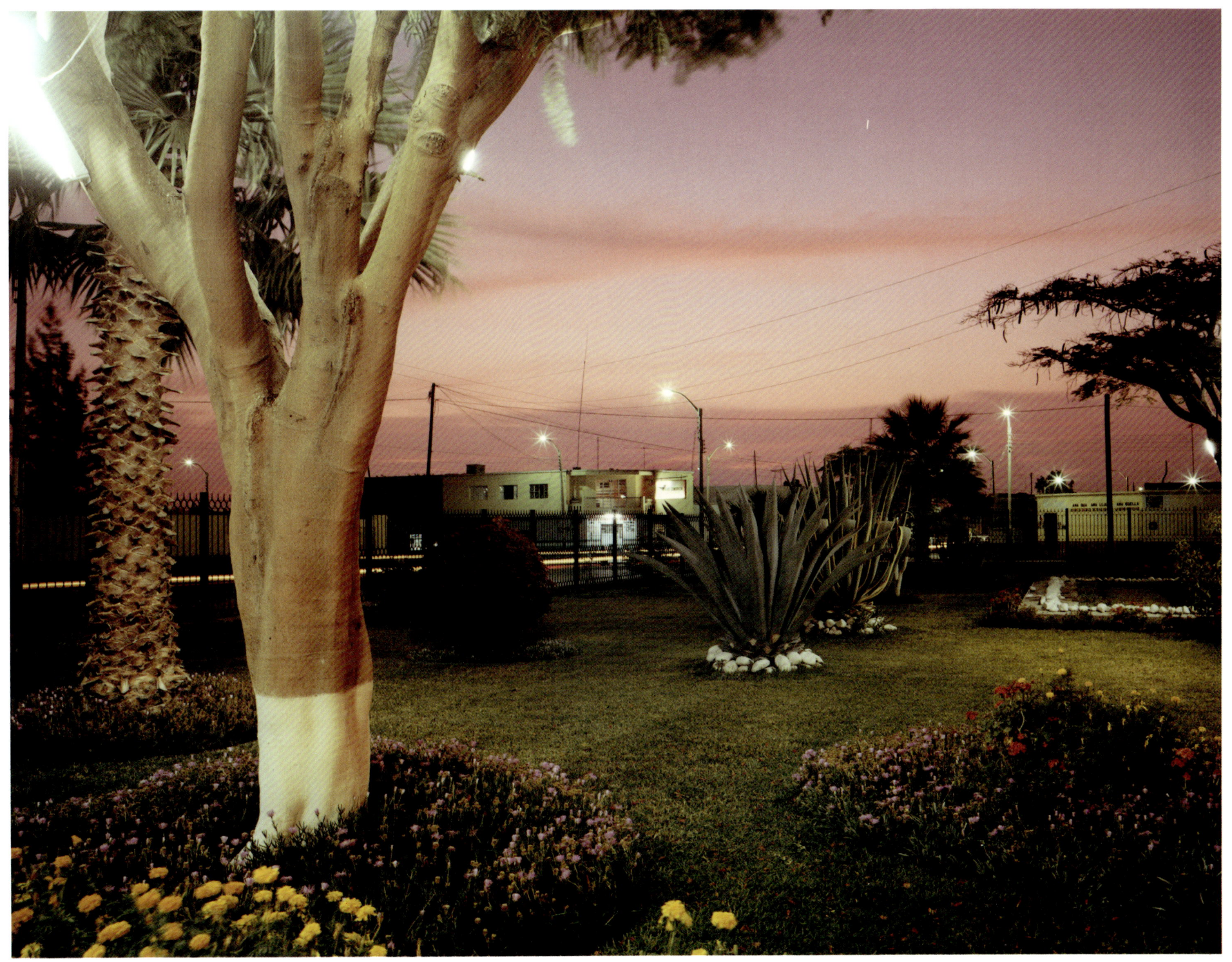

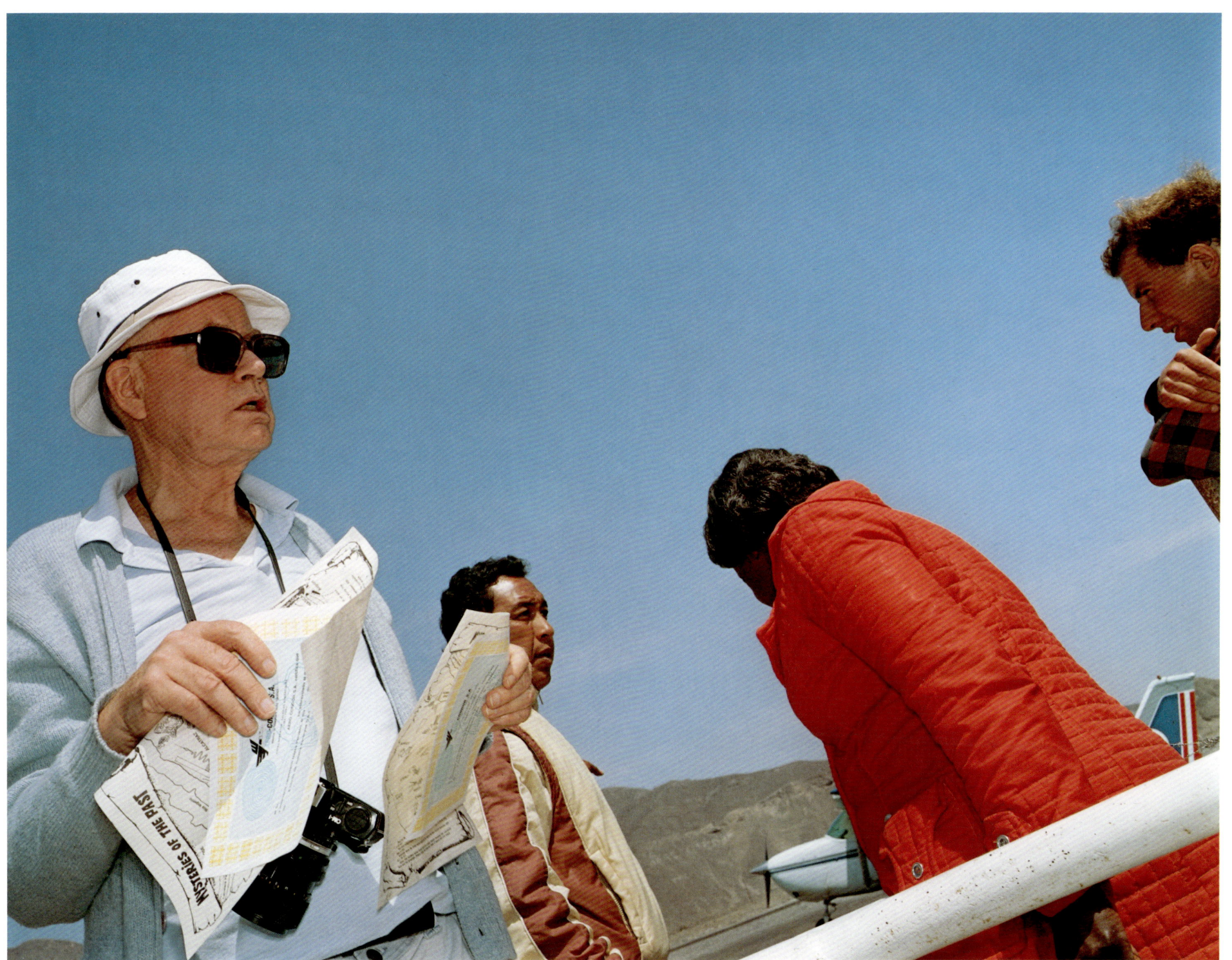

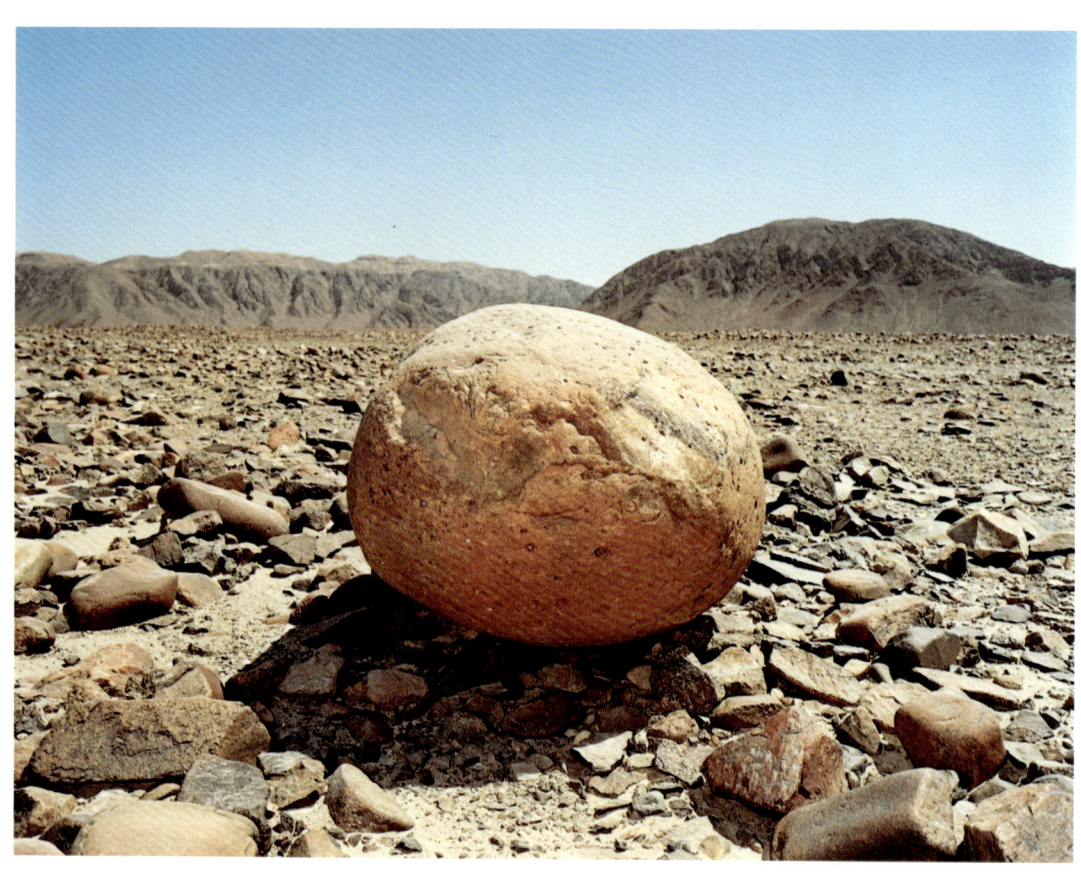

38 • RED ROCK EMBEDDED WITH FOSSIL ANIMALS

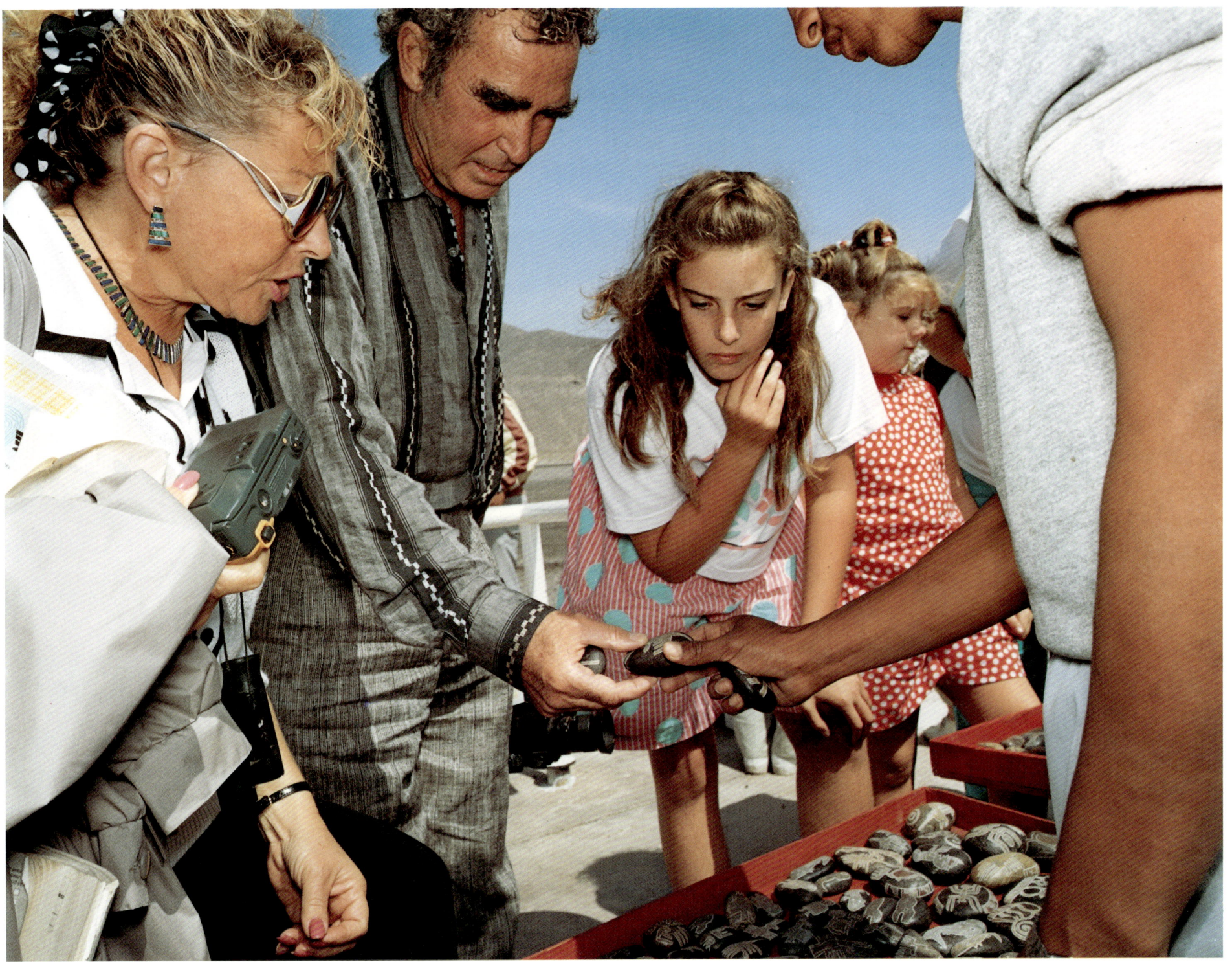

39 • CARVED STONES

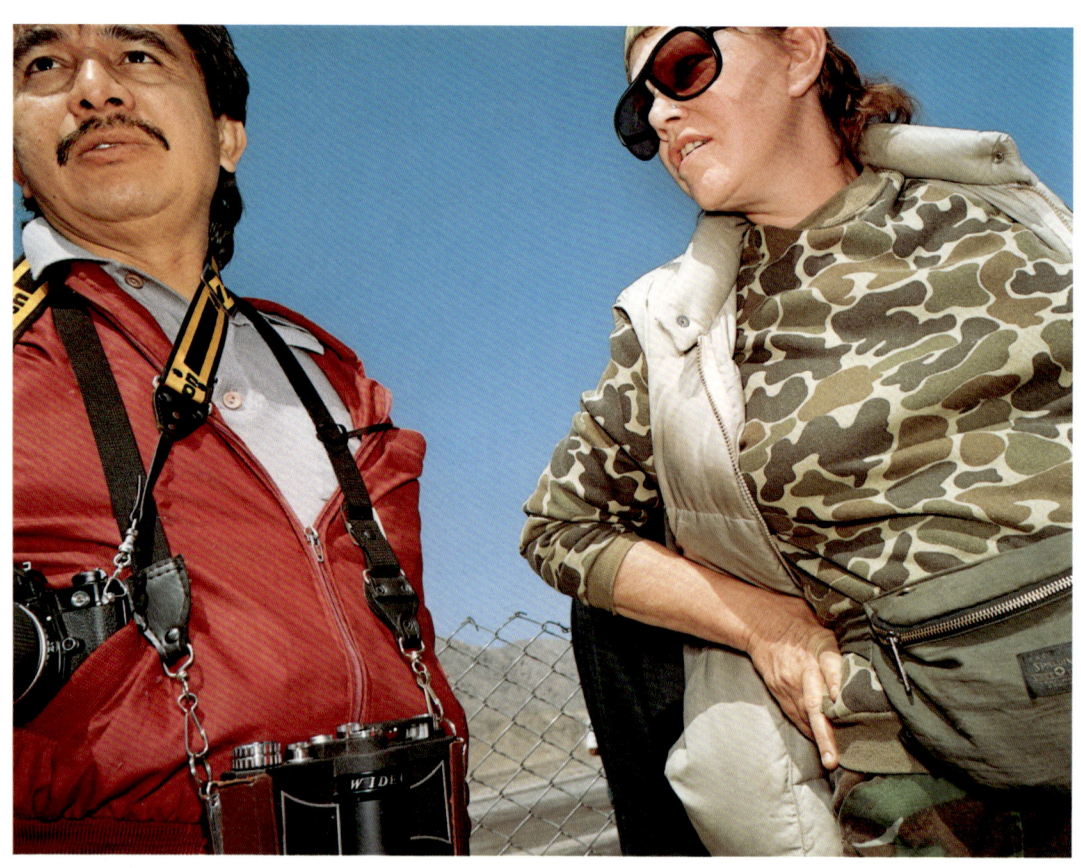

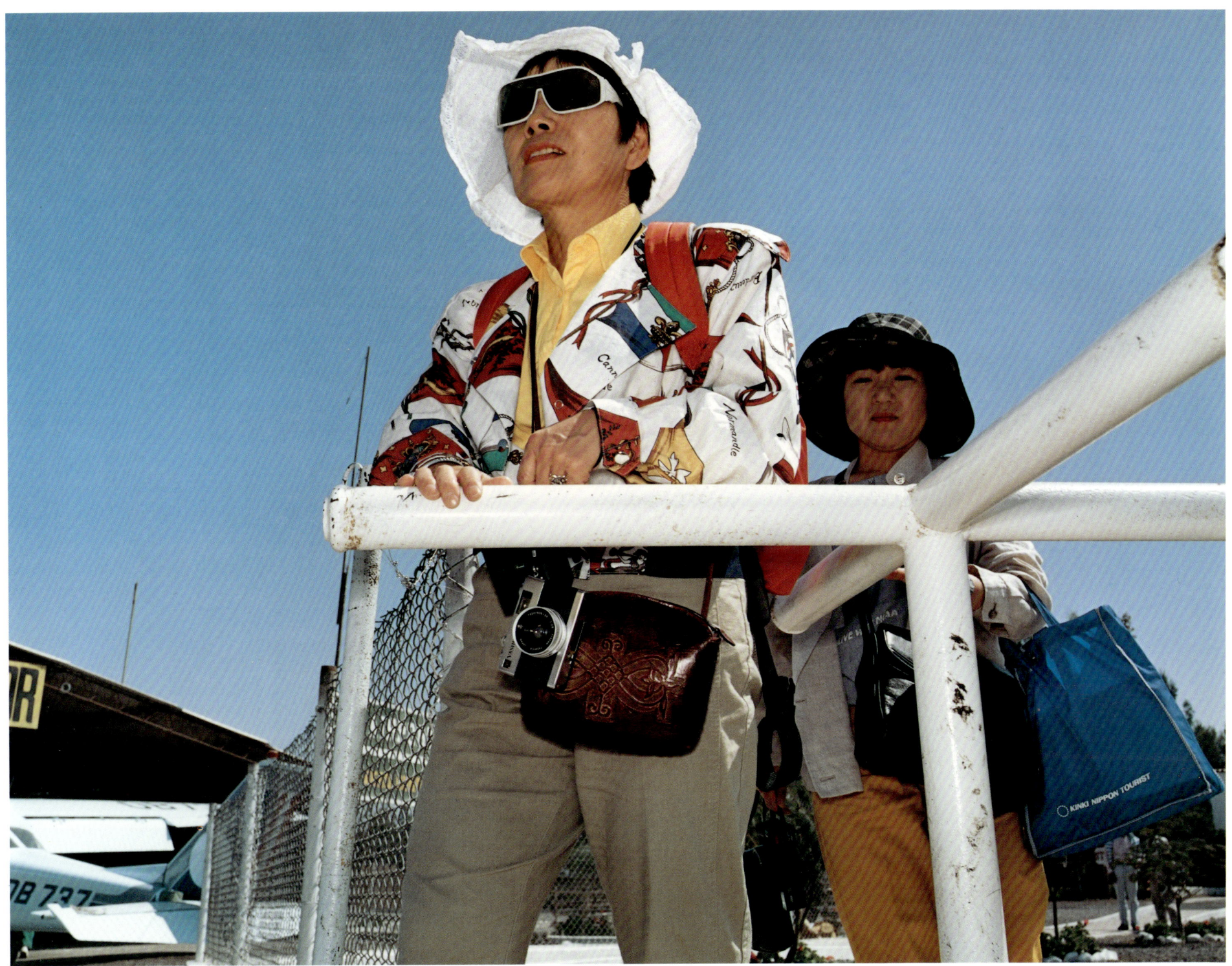

41 • 'KINKI NIPPON TOURIST'

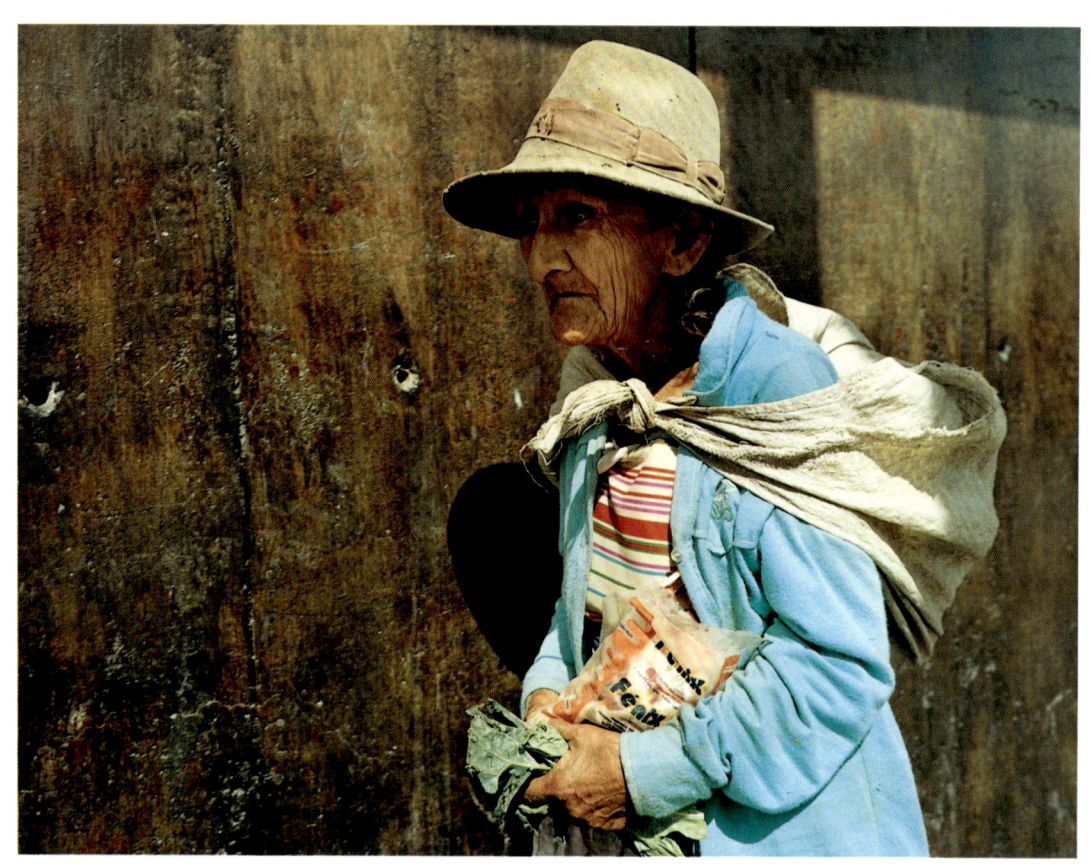

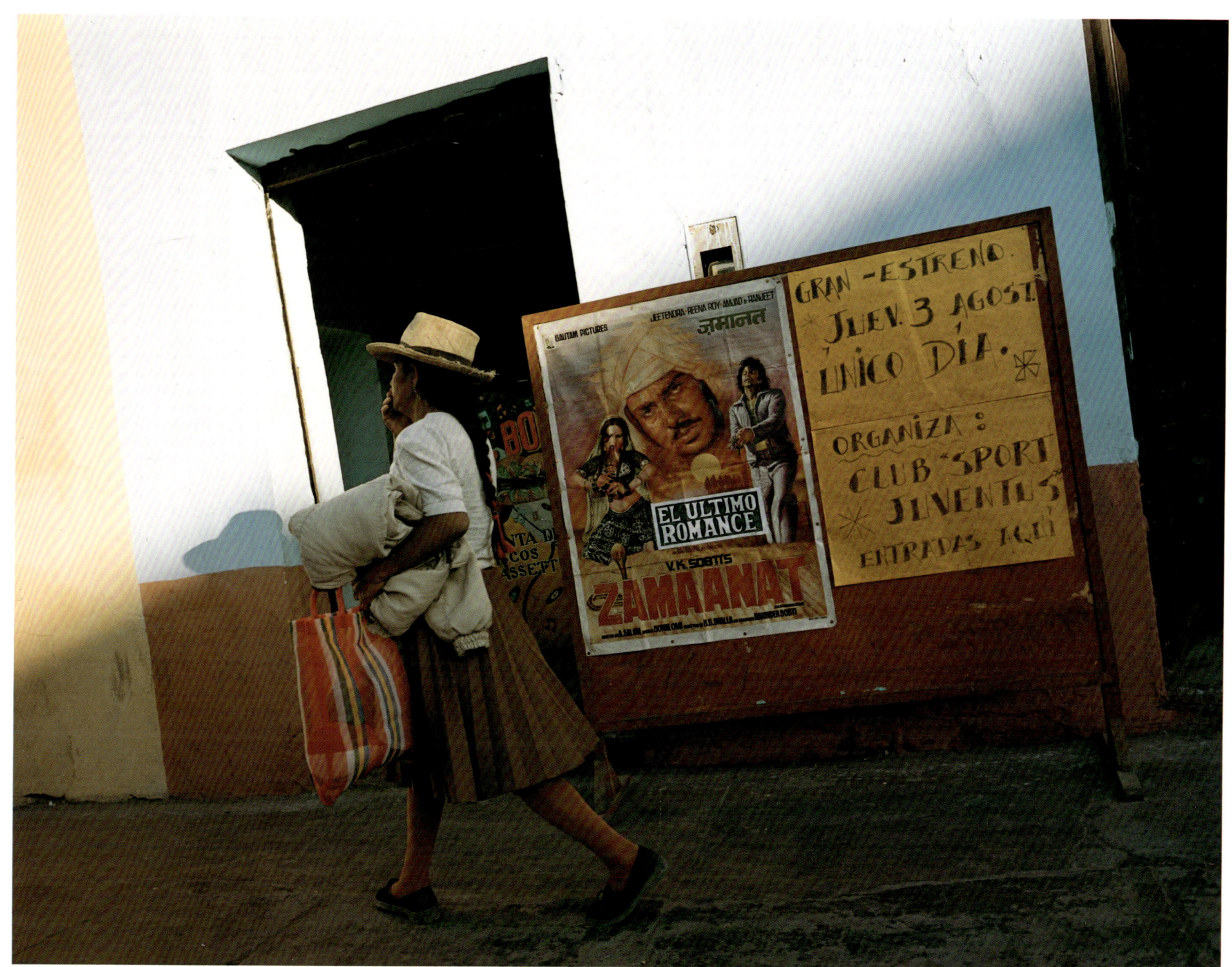

45 • 'The Last Romance'

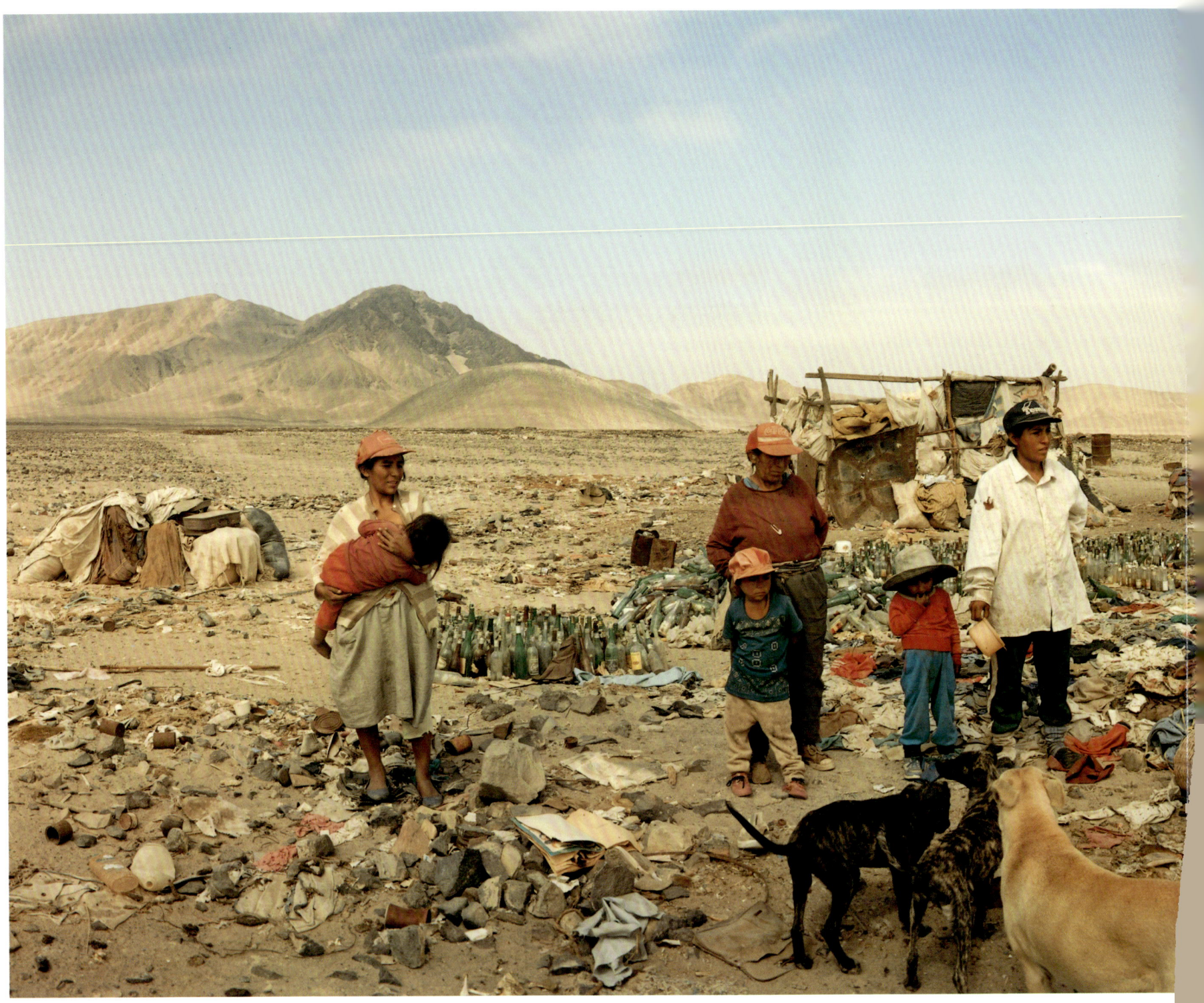

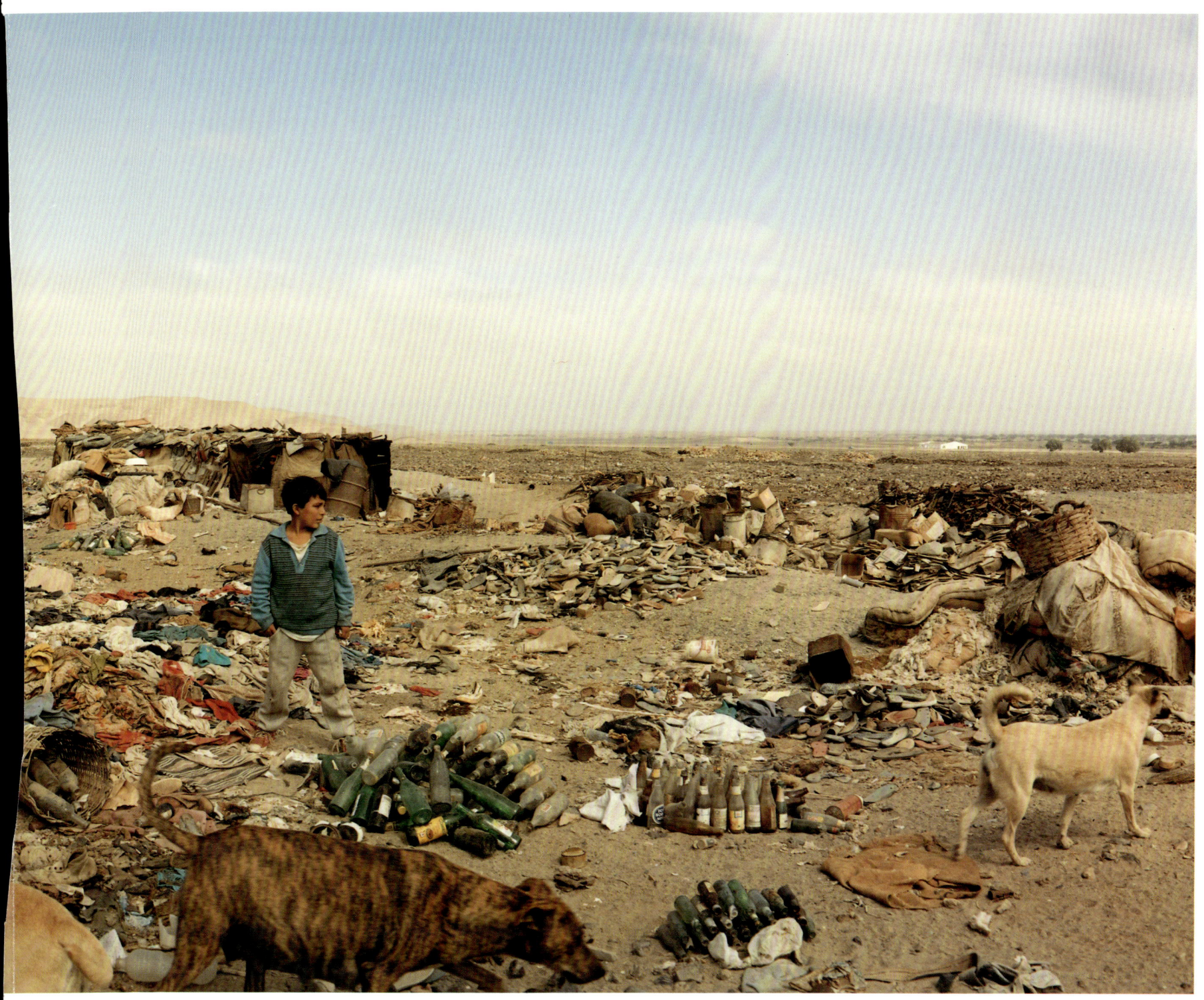

on Town Refuse Tip

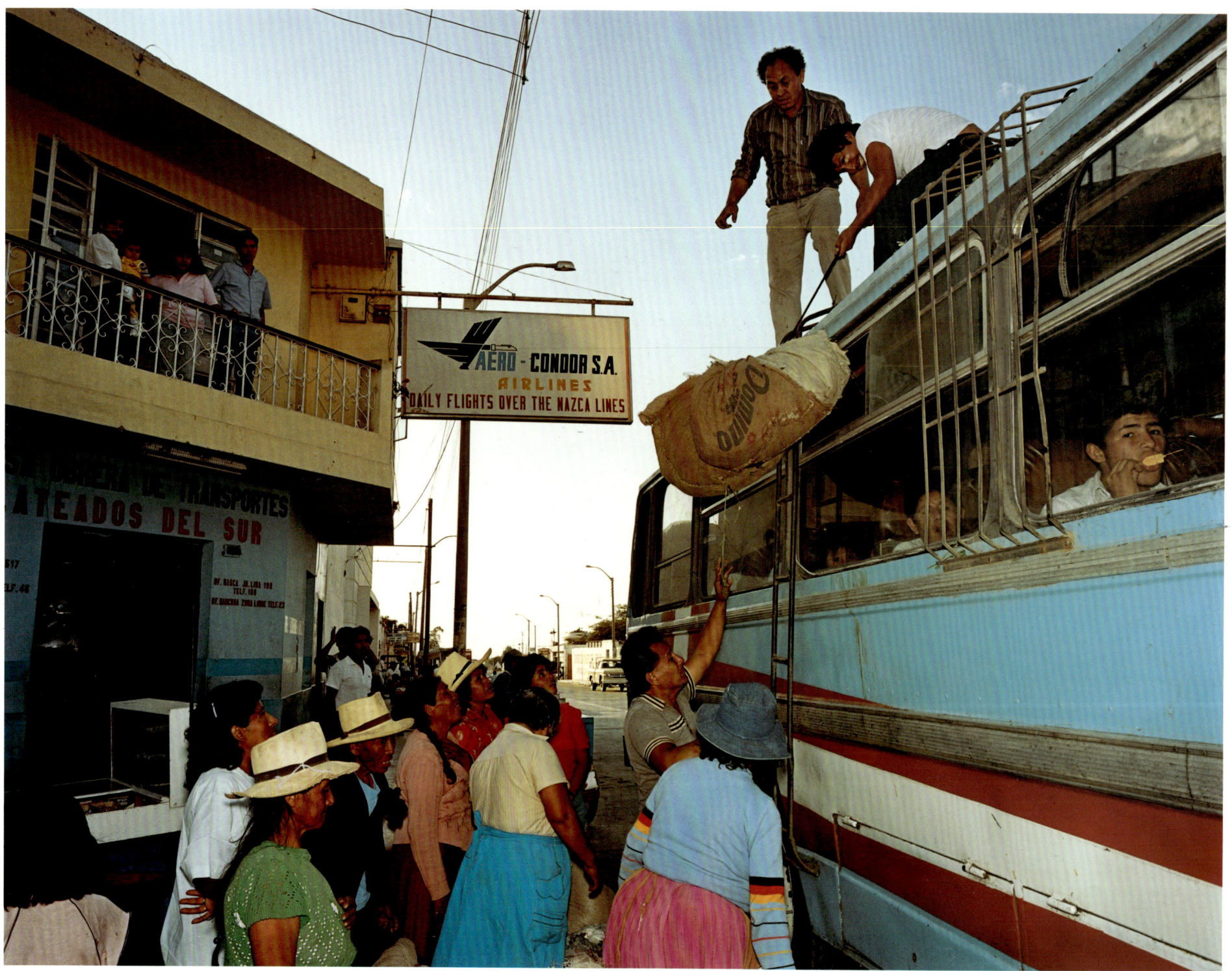

44 • BUS STATION

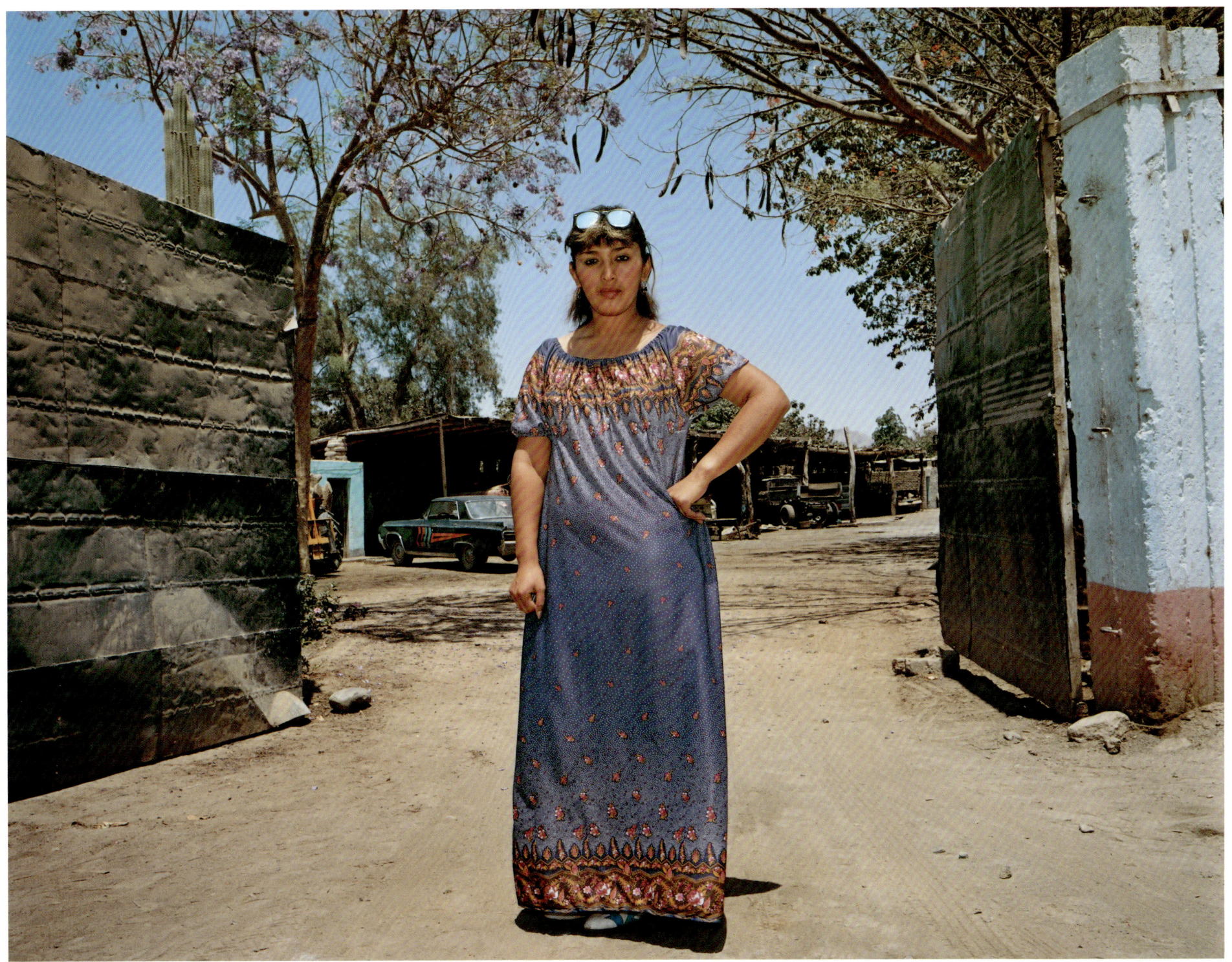

46 • GARAGE SECRETARY

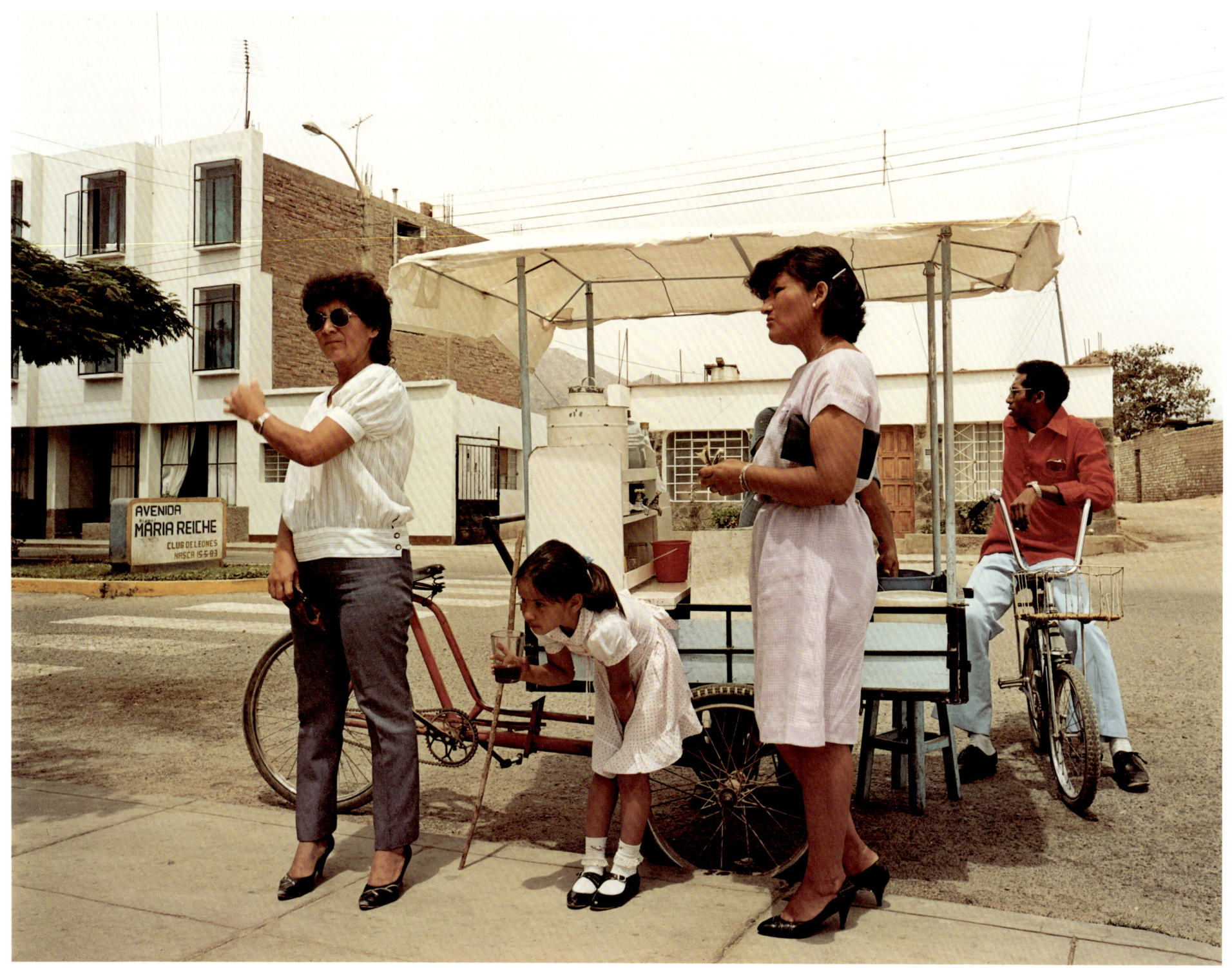

47 • Chicha Stall after Church on Sunday

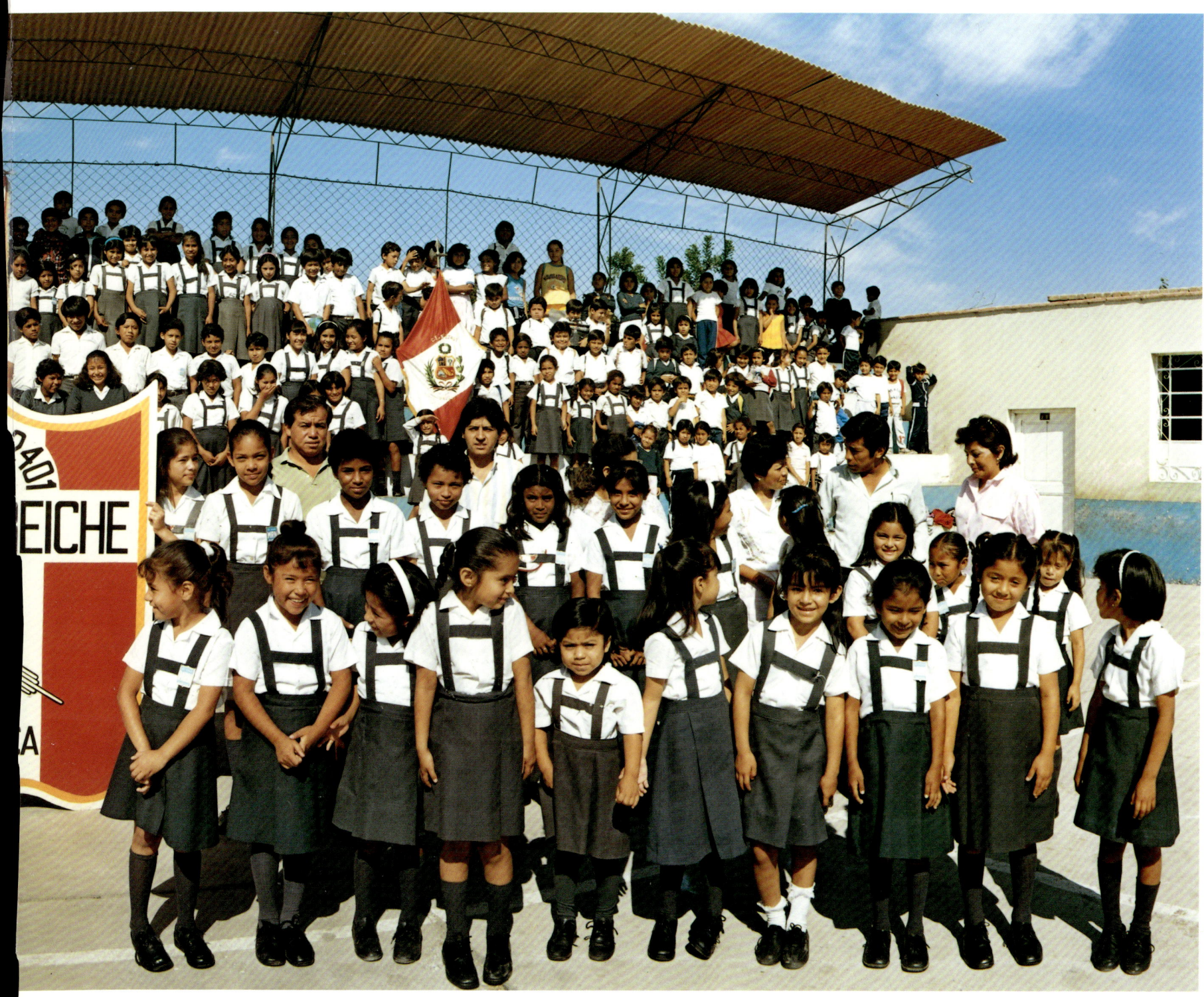

MARIA REICHE'

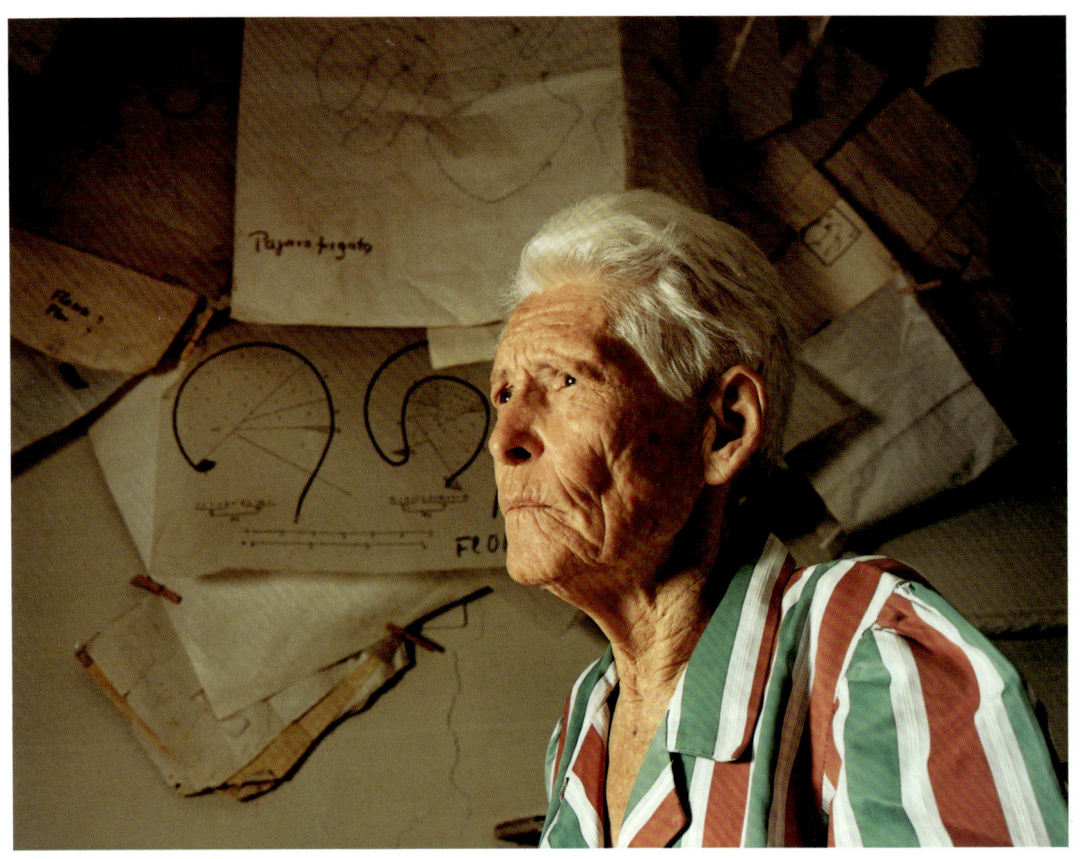

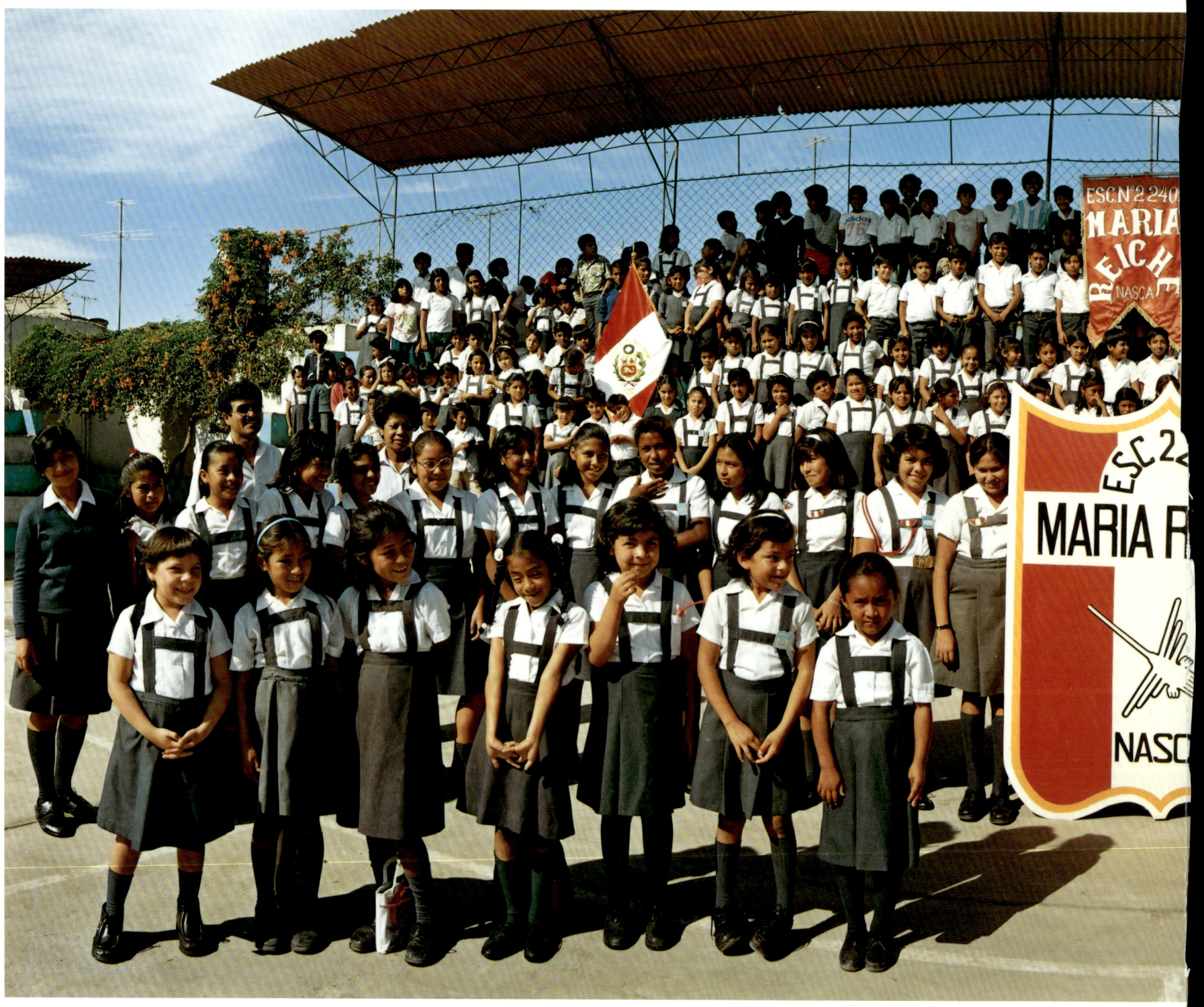

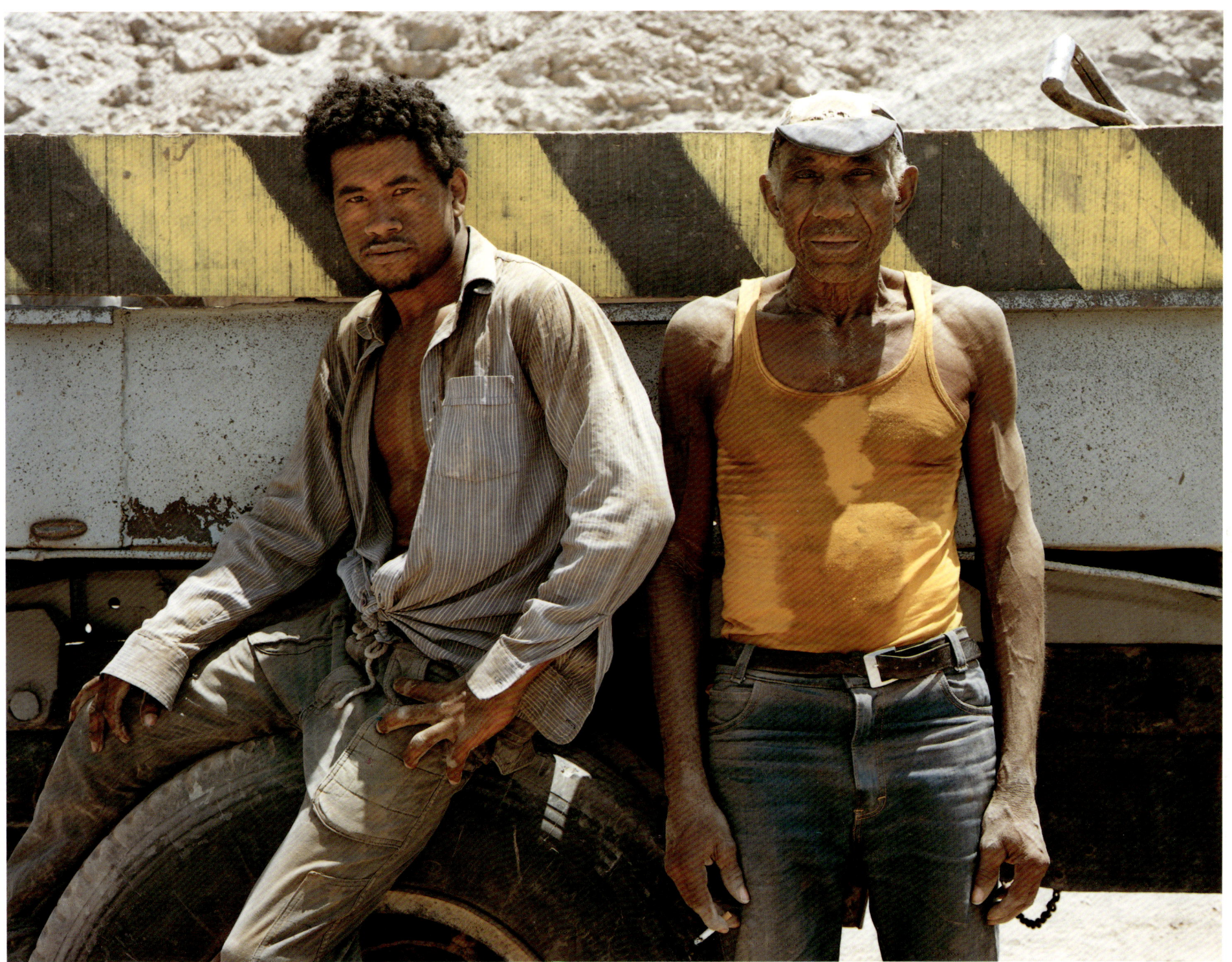

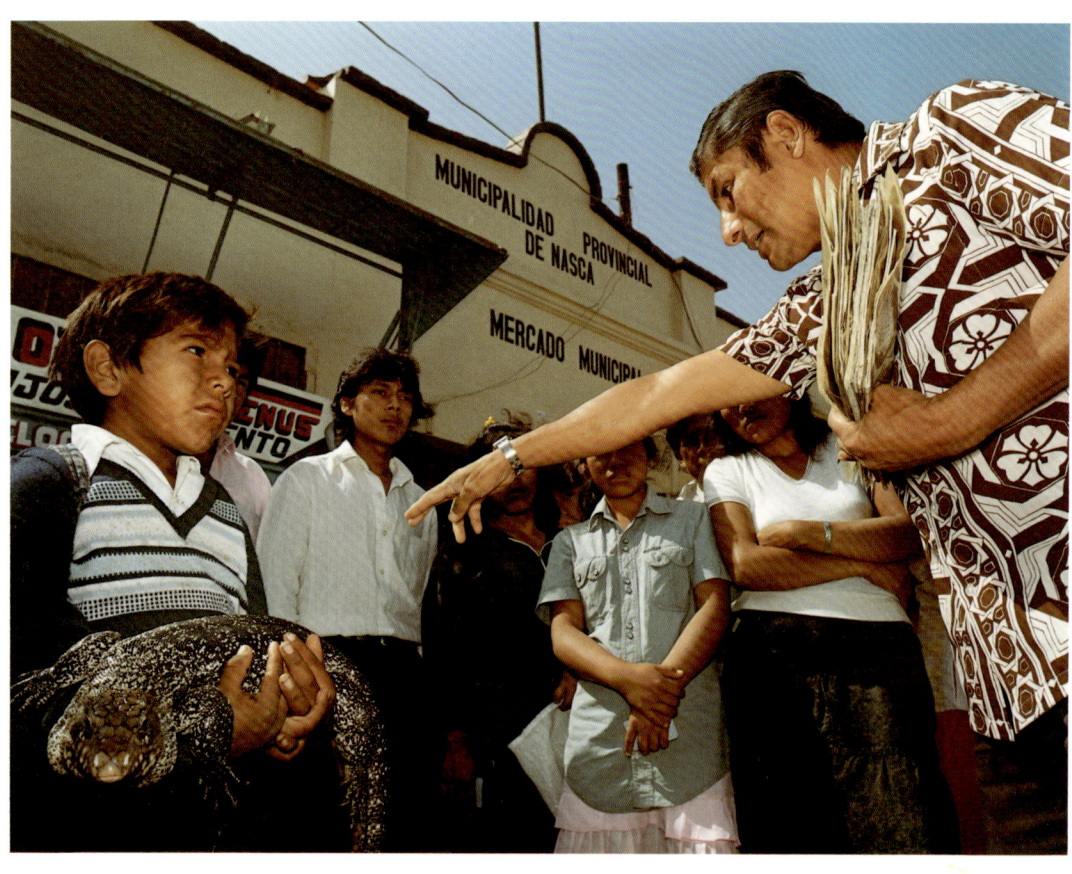

51 • 'Charlatan' (Seller of Folk Medicine)

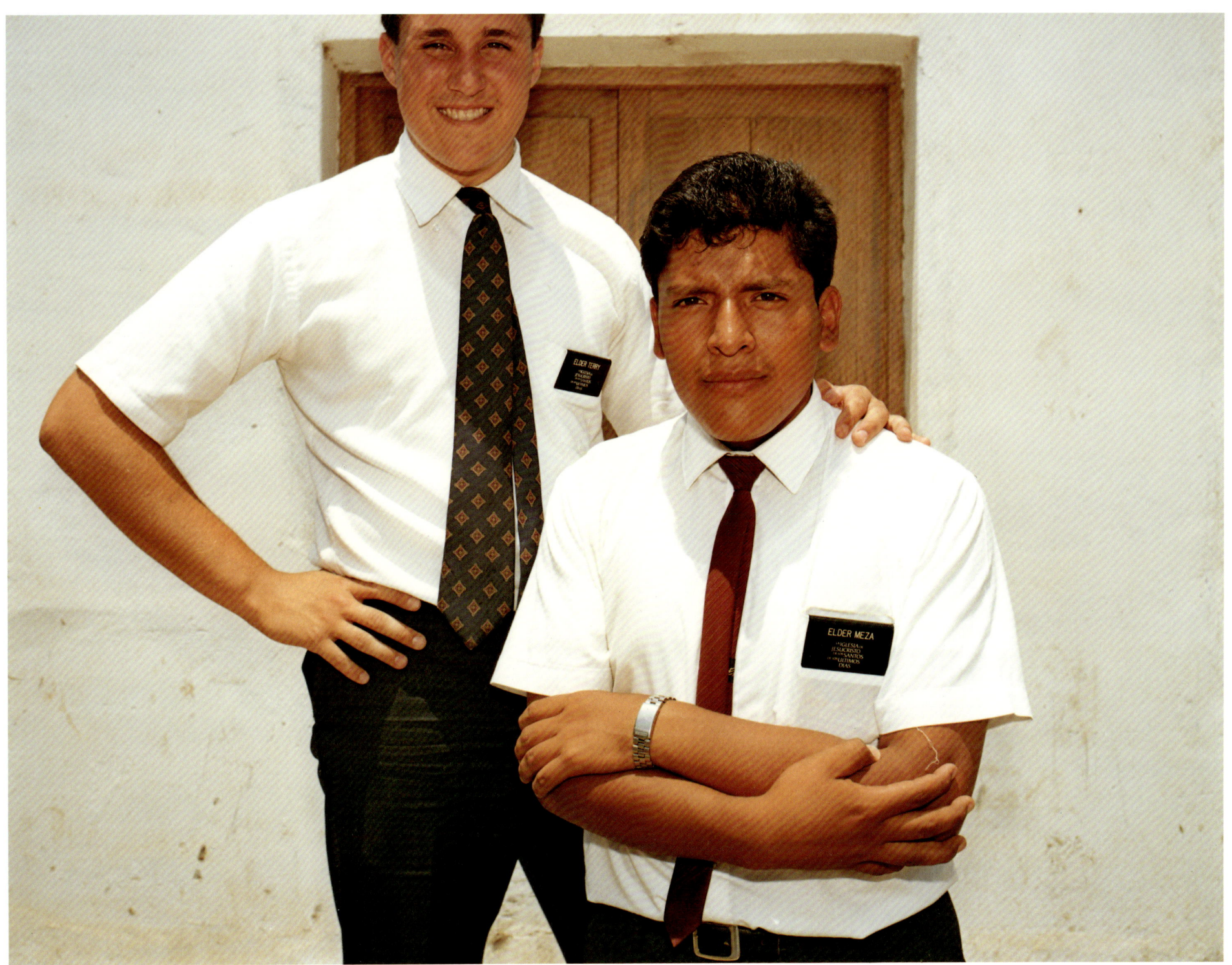

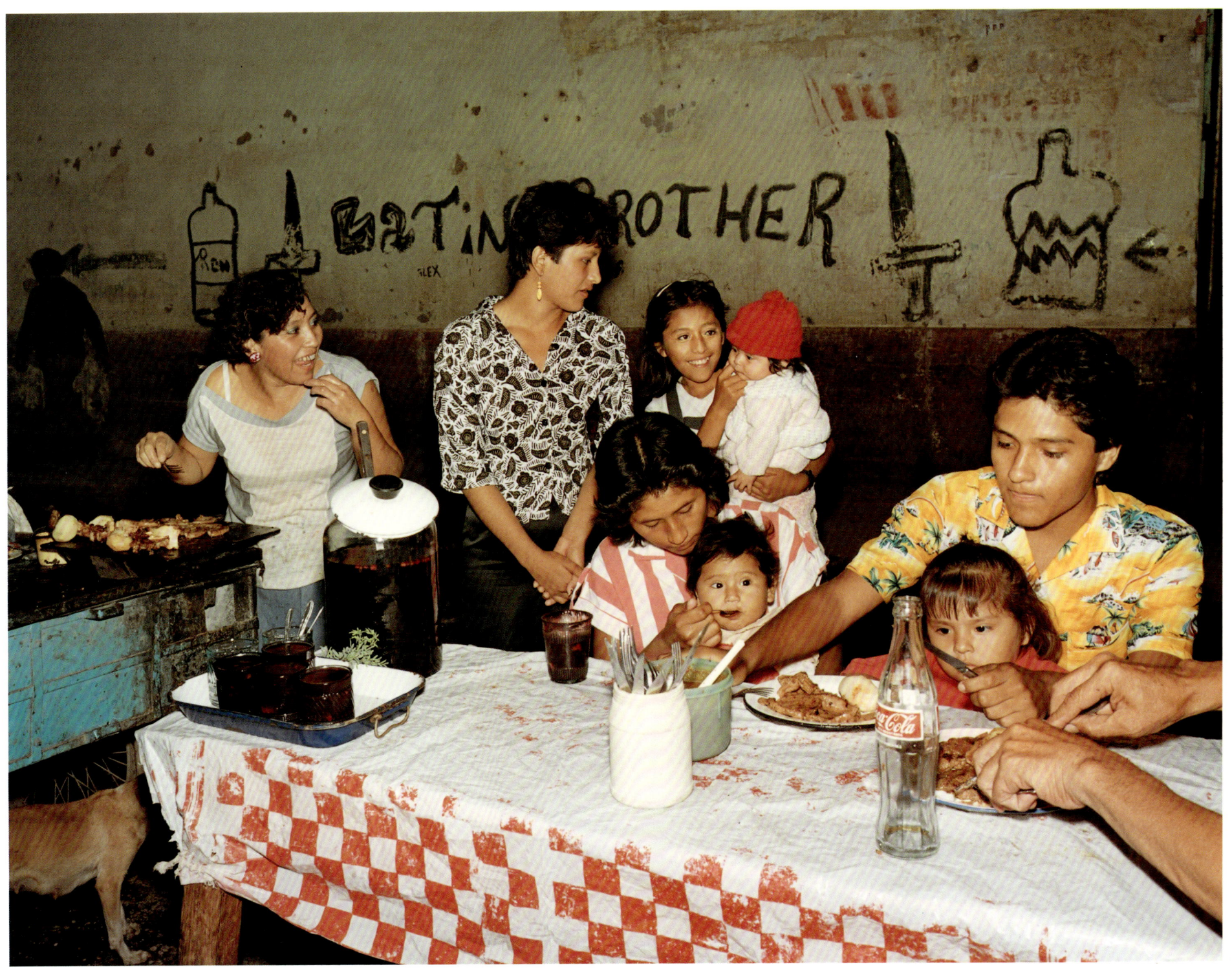

53 • 'LATIN BROTHER'

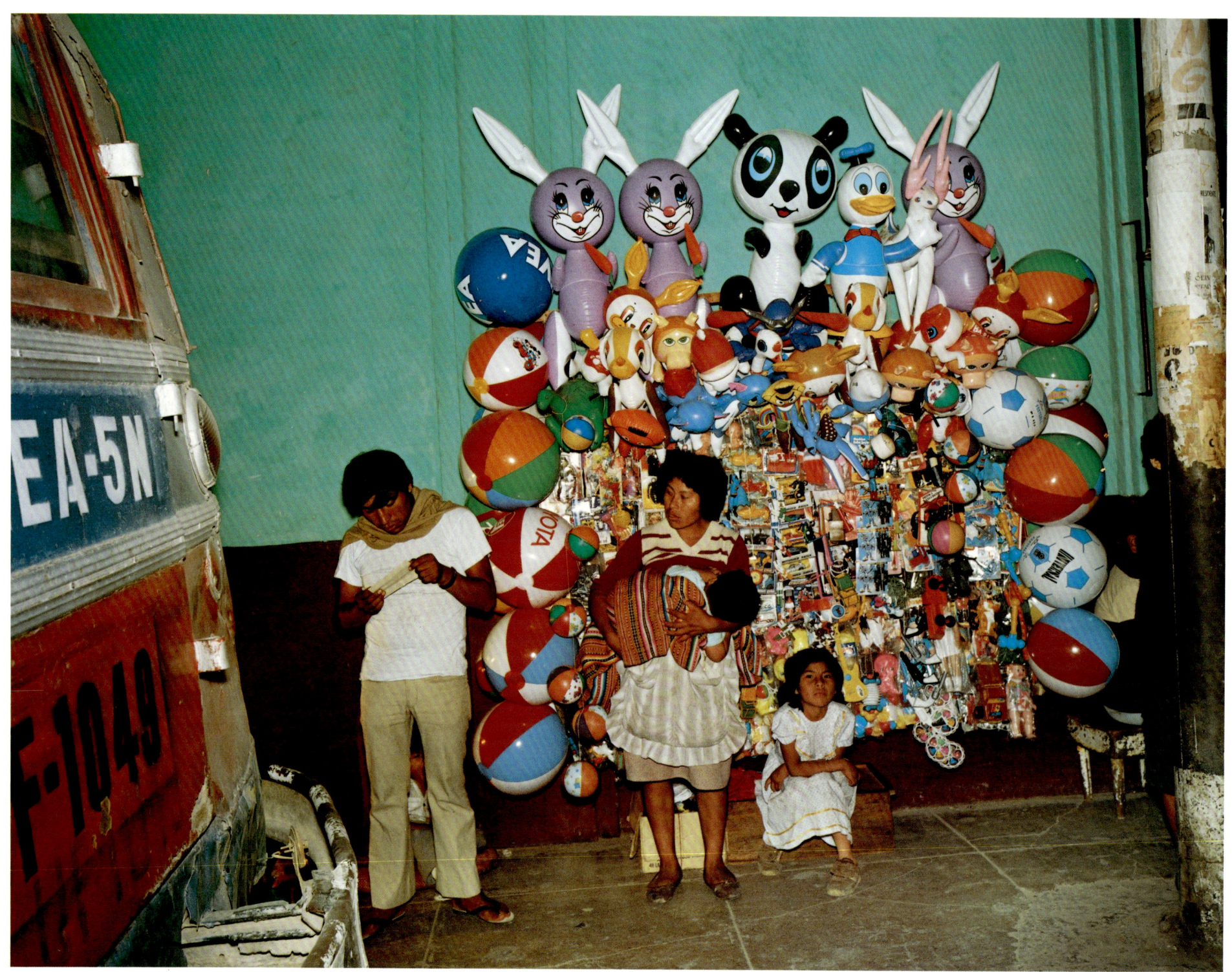

54 • TOY SELLER, CHRISTMAS EVE

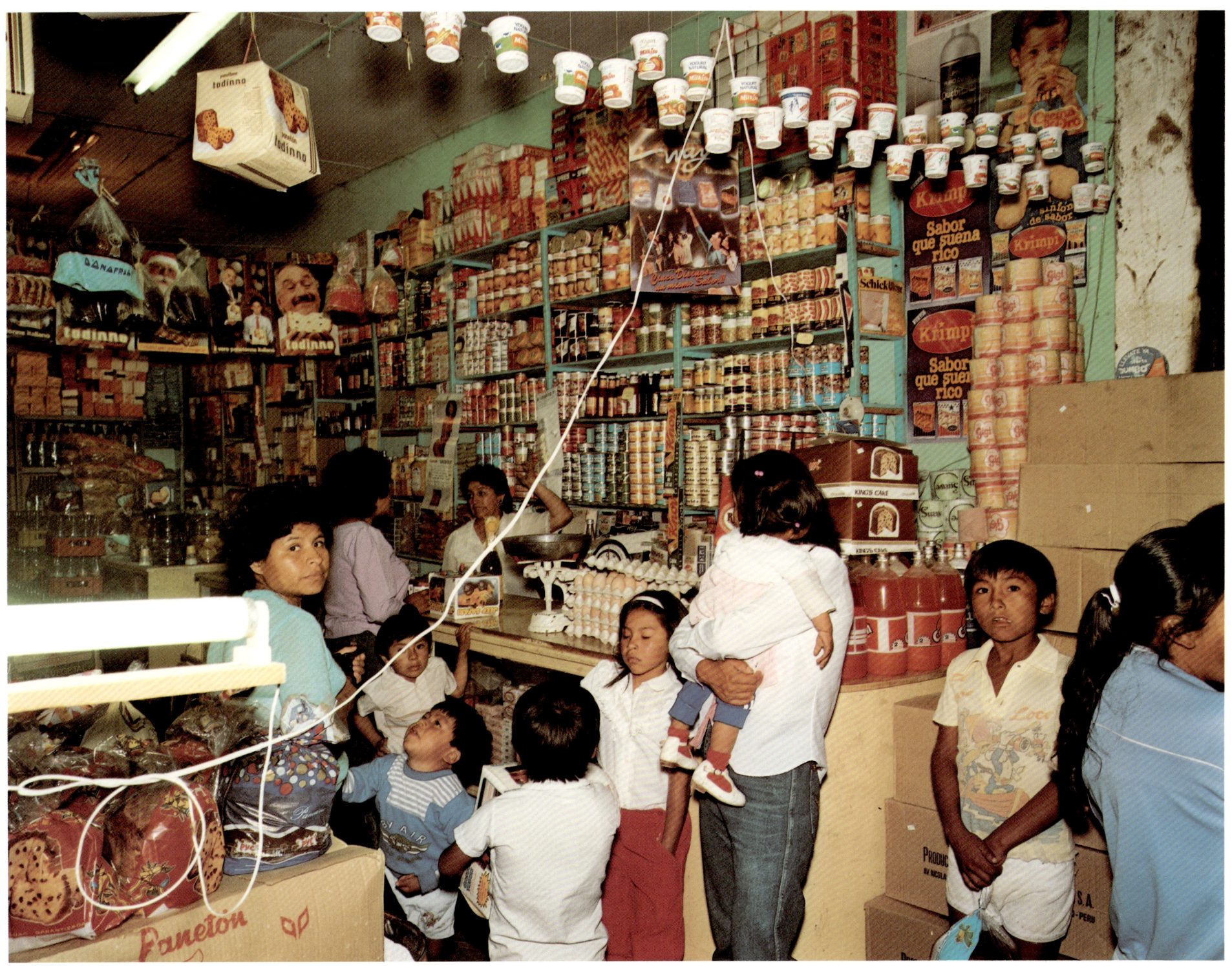

55 • GROCER, CHRISTMAS EVE

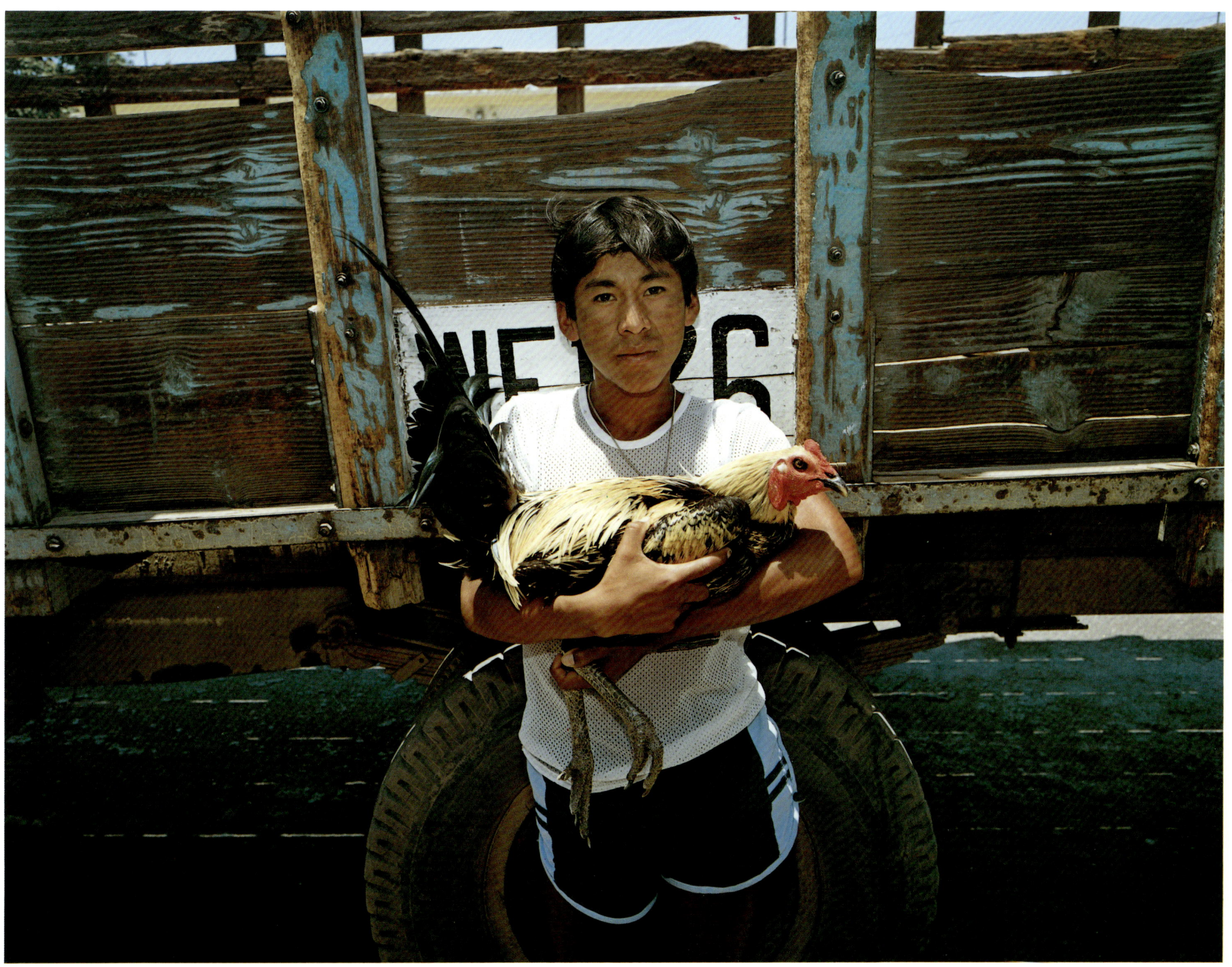

56 • BOY WITH FIGHTING COCK

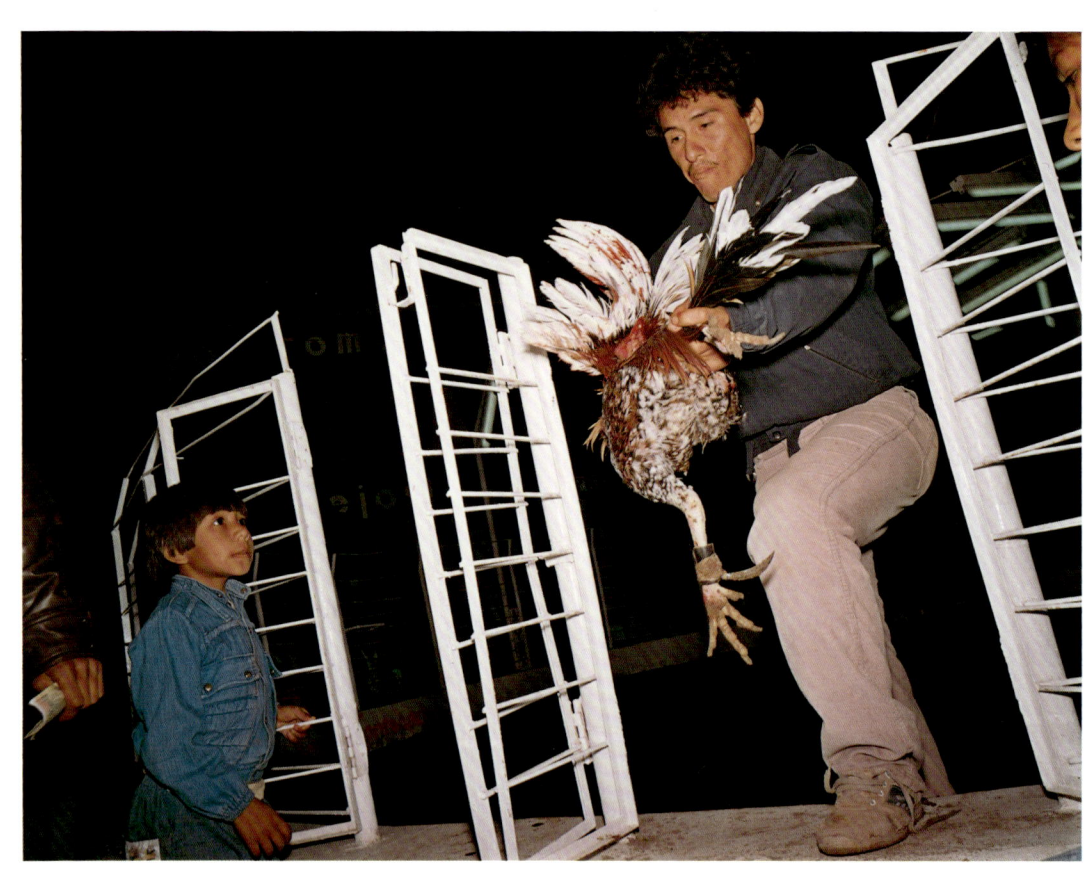

57 • Dead Bird with Spur

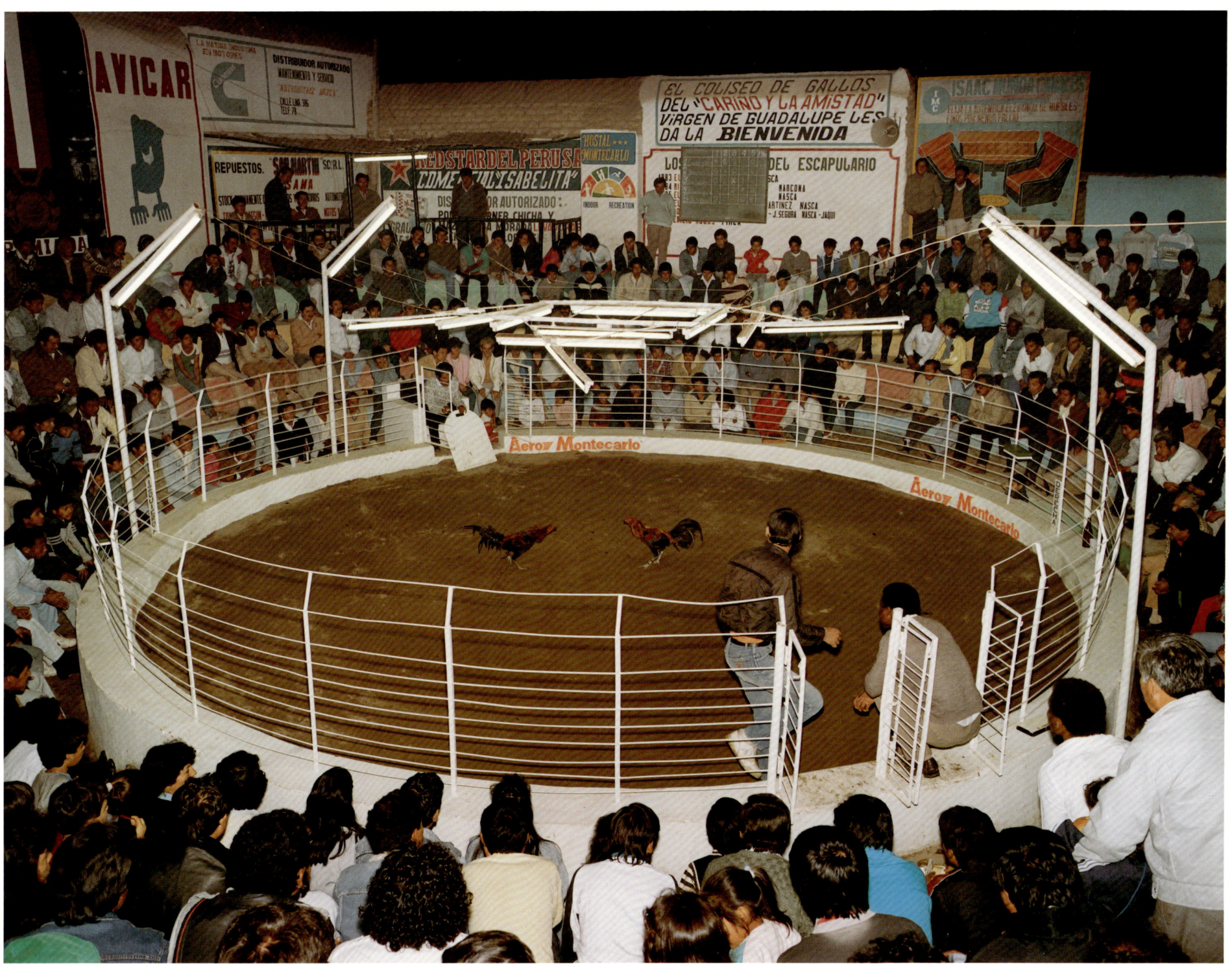

58•'El Coliseo de Gallos'

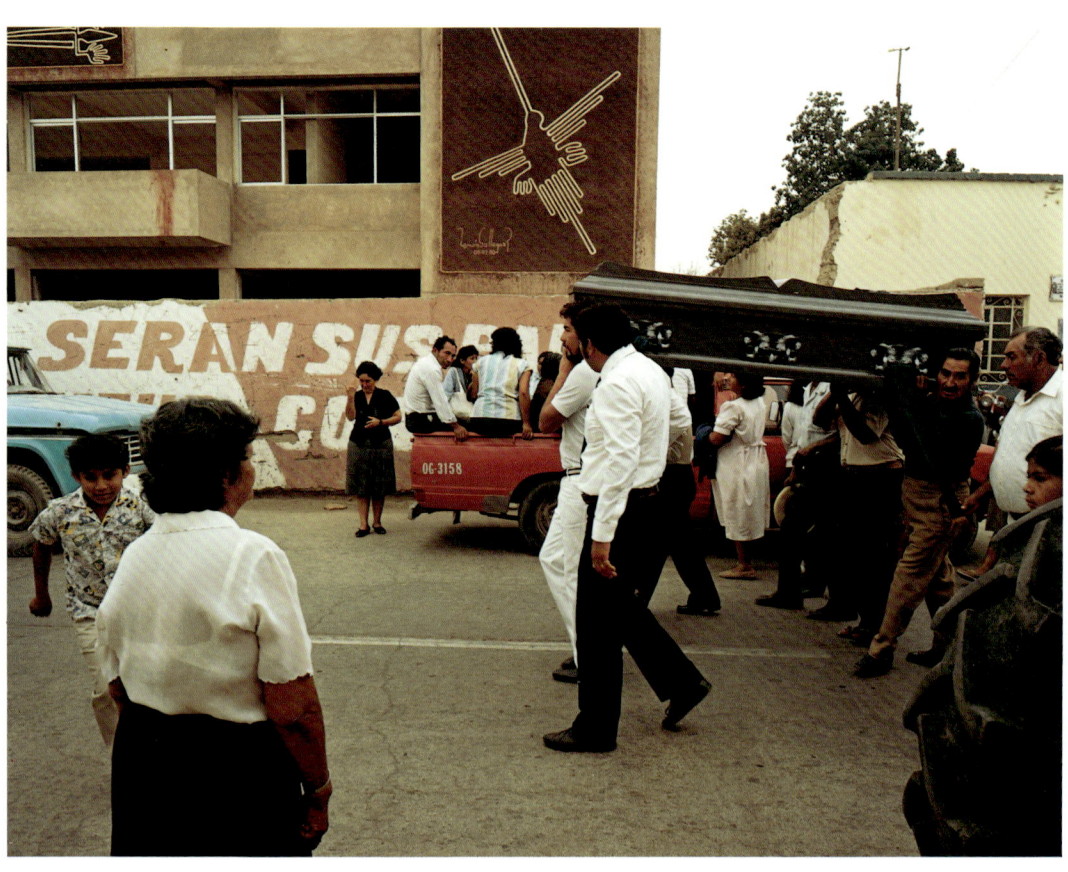

59 • PROCESSION PAST MUNICIPAL BUILDING

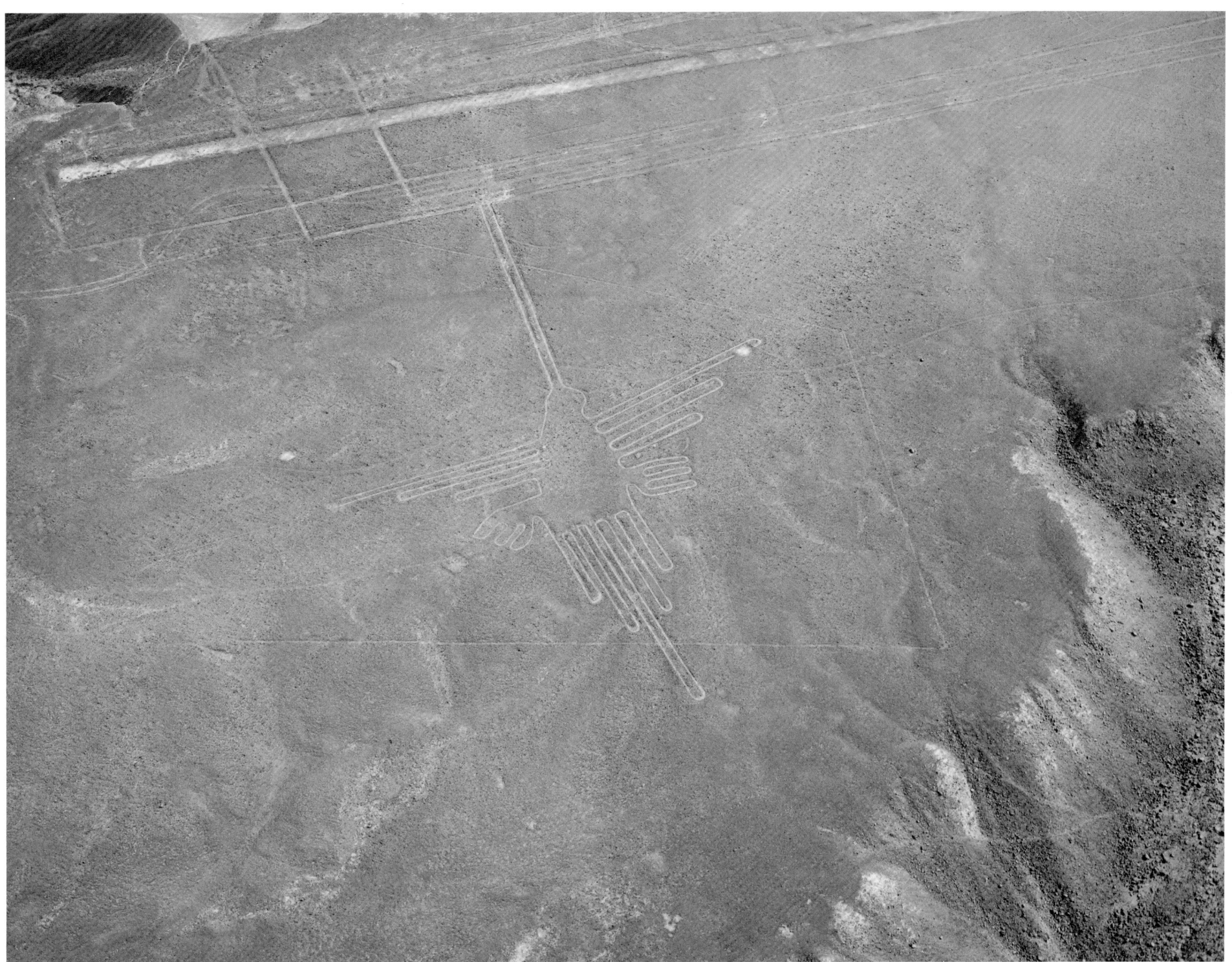

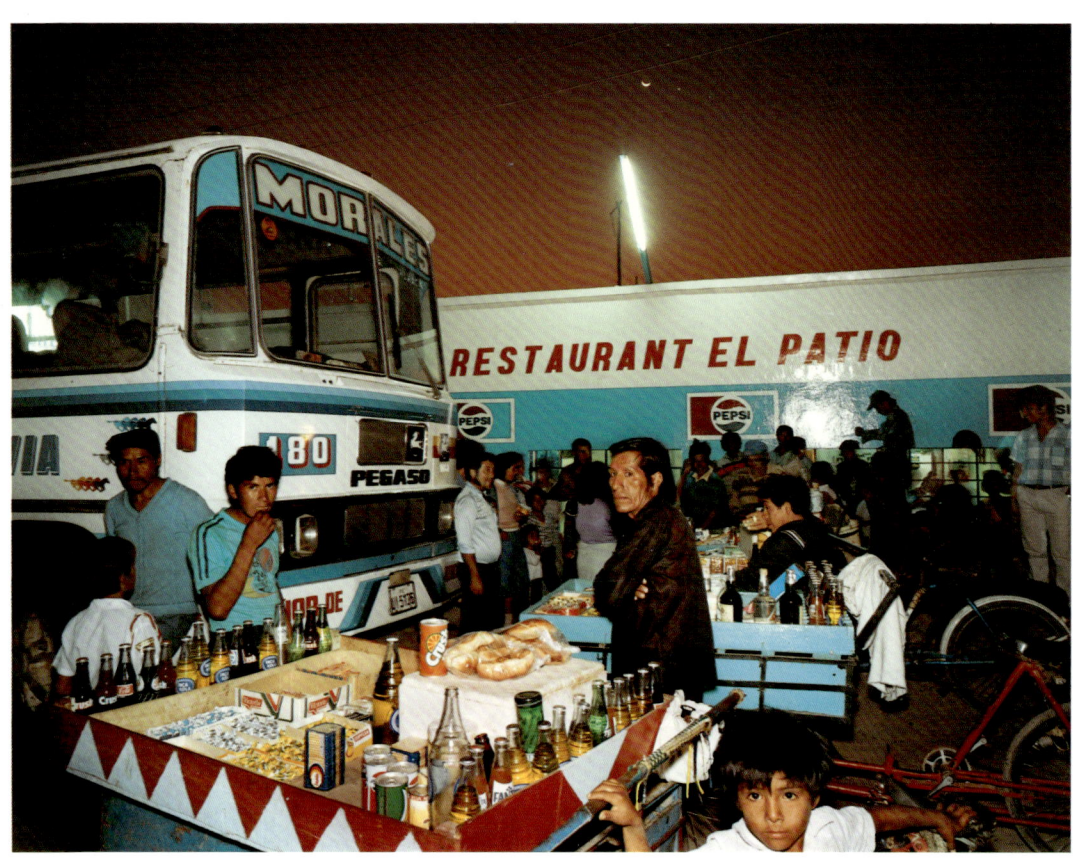

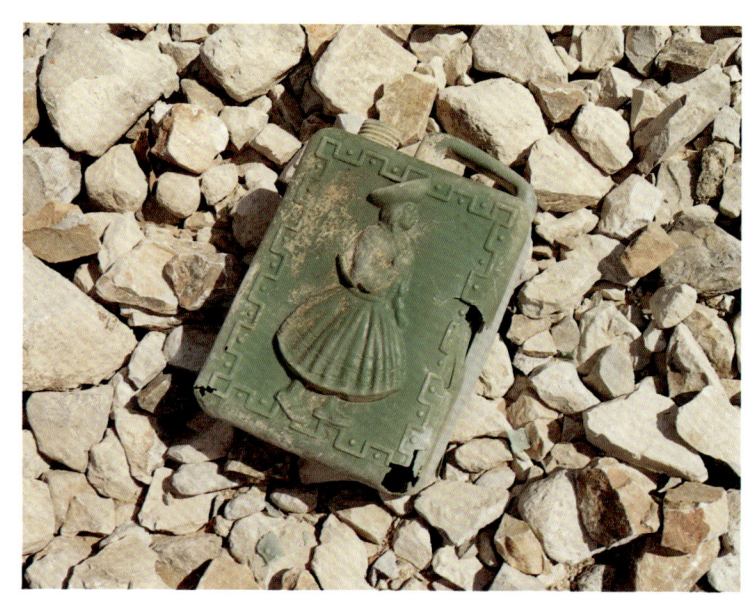

63 • KEROSENE CAN, REVERSE

I asked a child, walking with a candle,

'From where comes that light?'

Instantly he blew it out. 'Tell me where it is gone-

then I will tell you where it came from.'

Hasan of Basra

Hasan quote reproduced by
permission from *The Sufis* by Idries Shah
(Octagon Press Ltd., London)

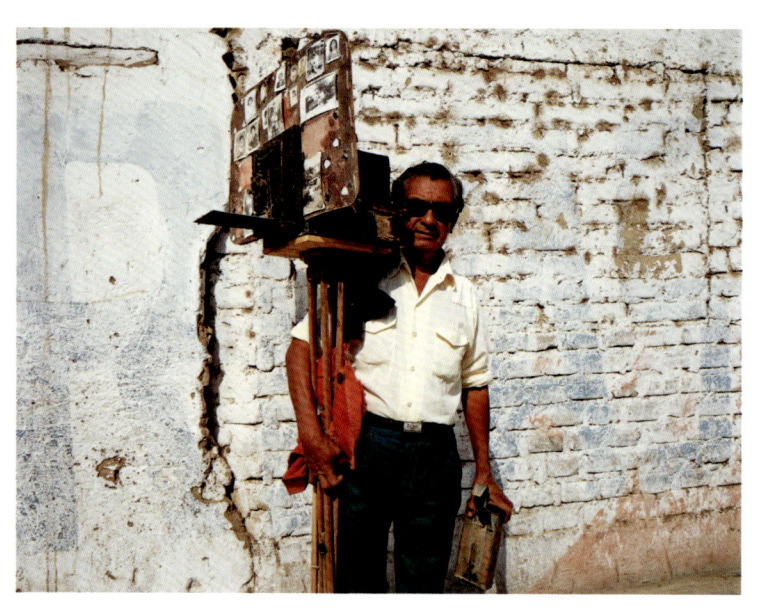

'Explicit description does not preclude richness, mystery, metaphor, or pathos. . . . . A sense of responsibilty to what is seen and felt transcends preconceptions of style. Vision becomes a moral act as photography modulates reality from the dimension of the actual to the synthesis of art.'

Sally Eauclaire

THE FIRST, AND PERHAPS THE most important point to be made about the photographs in this book is that they should be considered as constituent elements in a photographic work and not as a documentary essay upon a place and a society. This is not to say that these images do not reflect the material aspect of the world – they do so in a series of precise, contained, cohate delineations of surface and moment. Rather, it is to admit freely that the concept of the photographic document's veracity is as politically loaded and as treacherously complex as the clash of cultures depicted in the work.

David Parker's images are at once both less and more than a document. They have not been taken casually – snatched – by some itinerant journeyman, like so many photographs of the Third World, but have been *made* – carefully constructed and moulded into a collective, fluid narrative by a mind that professes the expressive intent of the artist.

One might be tempted to surmise, therefore, that Parker's imagery is concerned less with fact than with fiction, or that it is more fictional than factual, but that would be to oversimplify. Photography's teasing of realism's strands is more subtle (and problematical) than that. Instead, let us characterise Parker's mode as realist, his intent as poetic, his means provisional, and his goal........His goal, no less, is the expression of a truth - the truth, or mystery in question being how a literally superficial, monocular medium like photography can comment upon decidedly profound, multifarious issues like race, religion, art and history.

If the foregoing sounds somewhat portentous, we might illustrate Parker's ambitions by practical example. Consider what he has consciously eschewed, the kinds of imagery he *might* have made at Nazca, or at any other Third World site similarly blighted by the tourism of archaeology, such as Luxor or Petra.

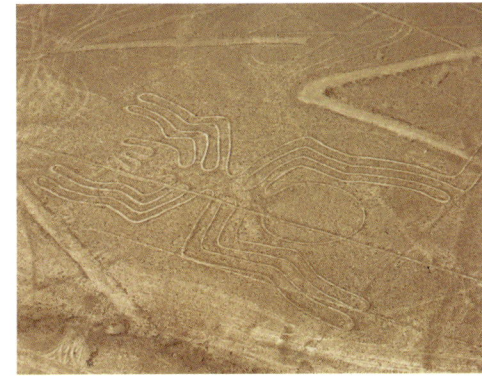

SPIDER

Firstly, there is the genre of the professional travel photographer, immediately denoted (with possibly unfairly perjorative undertones) by two words – "National Geographic." The keynotes of this mode are colour and exoticism, marked frequently by darkly dramatic landscapes and pseudo-anthropological studies of brightly costumed "natives." At its best, this kind of thing is superficial and unwittingly patronising. At worst, it is offensively voyeuristic and a dark reiteration of racist orthodoxies.

A less overtly offensive mode can be designated the 'arty archaeological', which, as the term suggests, concentrates upon the archaeological remains, stressing notions of mystery and universality. This 'Lost Kingdoms' approach tends to isolate the ancient artefacts in a picaresque frame, violently decontextualising them, but at least demonstrating a spiritual empathy with, if not understanding of, the culture which created them. However, such a strategy tends to marginalise, indeed wholly ignore the often parlous social plight of those who nominally have inherited these dubious cultural legacies.

For example, only after visiting Luxor did I realise that the ancient temple of Amun Re existed not in dignified isolation, but was crowded on all sides by a bustling, not to say hustling modern city, and tainted by an incessant tourist promenade, a violation marked by vicious mistrust and apprehension on all sides. To be sure, I had suspected this, but no visual record had prepared me for that reality, just as Marilyn Bridges' or Edward Ranney's exemplary views of the ancient sites could not have prepared David Parker for the realities of Cuzco or Nazca.

A third photographic approach which Parker might have adopted is that of the 'concerned photojournalist.' As the soubriquet suggests, the 'concerned' photographer evinces concern for the disenfranchised, particularly those of the Third World, and attempts to lay bare the economic exigences of post-colonial societies in order to tweak the conscience of the cosmopolitan elite. Unfortunately, in order to raise an effective counter voice amidst all those shrilly promulgating the dominant ethos of capitalist consumerism, the photographer is forced to compete in the hard sell stakes. Therefore the imagery

91

of concerned photography in the mass circulation periodicals has degenerated frequently into a kind of hard sentimentality, whereby a battery of visual devices culled from art history — chiaroscuro being the all-time favourite — are employed to exaggerate, heighten, and provoke the desired response. It has become, all too often, an imagistic 'cry wolf'.

Such breast beating, however skilled and subtle, tends toward an end result that is superficial and overdetermined. Even if good propaganda, it perhaps makes bad art. If good art, its propagandist potential can be severely limited. This is not to say that art and propaganda are mutually exclusive, but in the realm of journalistic photography, a true synthesis of the two is rare enough to be devoutly cherished.

Without disparaging further these established genres, for each in its turn has engendered memorable bodies of work, we can say that Parker's game is more complex. That game certainly embraces art before propaganda, although Parker evinces a strong empathy with the people of Nazca, and maintains a discreet yet insistent political commentary throughout the work. However, in these thoroughly postmodern times, he is acutely aware of the paradoxical role of photographic imagery — of any imagery for that matter — within our society. Thus, in keeping with a medium that seems to reek of ambiguity, that fluctuates violently between extremes of factuality and expressiveness, the meanings of Parker's pictures are as difficult to pin down as the *raison d'etre* for those enigmatic desert lines.

That is one reason why Parker heartily dislikes the term 'documentary' when ascribed to his work. Another is that it loads the imagery unnecessarily with an external moral weight, predetermined by others, and also suggests that all facts within have been presented with an equal meticulousness and apparent emotional distance.

The latter is patently not so. A cursory glance through Parker's carefully sequenced programme of images will reveal a concern with far more than anthropology or sociology. Aspects of the divine, the sublime, and the metaphysical are to be found amongst the tawdry third-hand Americana and the banal detritus of the baited tourist trap. A fine individual example can be seen in Parker's ghastly Mount Rushmore of four

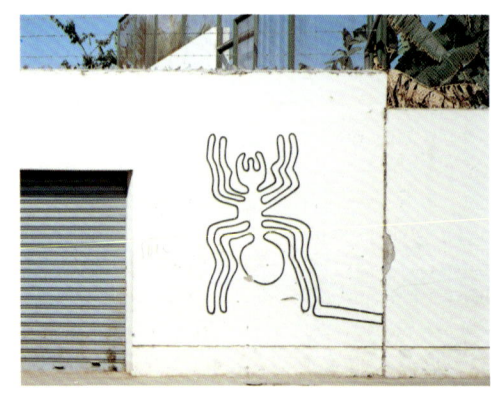

HOTEL WALL

skulls. The image refers to mortality and temporality — certainly — but the droll Rushmore illusion is as neat a pricking as any of the pomposity of nations which are seen to harbour grandiose colonialist ambitions and effect a lofty disregard for the forces of nature.

Parker, perhaps more contentiously, eschews pure documentary because that, for him, "is not a photographic issue." He has rejected images for this book that were replete with information, and may have added richly to the narrative at a certain level, simply because they "weren't interesting images". What does he mean by this? Parker certainly is no out-and-out formalist, though like any serious photographer he is concerned that his images are cleanly and precisely structured. But if pressed upon this vexed question he would reply that photographic issues are comparable to musical or literary issues. In short, a good photograph is as ineffable as a piece of good music, a passage of good writing or painting.

Another way of putting it is to say that there must be a balance between form and content, and also between intellect and intuition. In this particular context the photographer's express intent is to extend beyond the purely documentary, to mould the image so that it not only *records* what the camera sees, but in the process *expresses* what Parker wants to say. In short, the photographer's task on site is to intuit the form for the content, and then during the long, essential task of editing and sequencing, consciously define and refine that content which has been divined, provisionally squeezed out of the hurly burly of the taking situation. Each image that ends up in this book, therefore, has been subject to a number of different thought processes and tested in various ways, against a standard that itself is subject to constant scrutiny, revision and modulation.

David Parker is another of those visual artists who have chalked up a debt to T. S. Eliot in the titling department. *Broken Images* is an excellent, richly connotative title for this work, alluding both to Parker's subject and to his medium. It certainly characterises the nature of the Nazca Lines themselves, images displaced totally from their primary context. The original cultural purpose of the Lines has been lost or forgotten. Today, they are violated or appropriated — both physically and symbolically — by at least five distinct vested interest groups — by the largely uncomprehending tourists, by the undoubtedly caring, but fiercely proprietorial archaeological academics, by the Peruvian heritage industry, by a number of sharp local entrepreneurs, and by the *campesinos,* the 'true' inheritors of the legacy.

The latter may well be the most compromised group of all. As distanced from their ancient ancestors as they are from their *gringo* visitors, their interest in the Lines is purely pragmatic. It is a 'natural' interest, the exploitation of an economic resource, rather than the preservation of a cultural heritage. Although the Nazcans may plaster the pictographic images over buildings, vehicles, bus stops, commercial literature, T-shirts, and tourist souvenirs, they are as displaced from the mystic power of the Lines as the basest tourist. And in a terrible irony, few of those who cause this imagistic rash to break out everywhere in the town have seen the pictographs as they were intended to be seen — from the lofty viewpoint of the Gods. Only the wealthy local flight operators and those fair skinned gods known as 'millonarios' can afford the thirty minute twirl over the *pampa* in a silver winged chariot.

Photographs also are broken images, interruptive fragments of actuality, images whose meanings constantly slip and slide — like those of the Lines — between the pragmatic and the expressive. Therein lies the element that continually eludes us, and thus continues to fascinate us.

Paradox lies at the heart of photography and, close by, ever appreciative of a good paradox, lurks irony, *the* expression par excellence of contemporary art. David Parker's gaze is essentially ironic, yet remains almost entirely free of cynicism. The Lines have cast their spell upon him. At the root of his report - roots which assuredly clutch tenaciously - lies the lesson of the Lines, the lesson of art and religion, the lesson of spiritual as opposed to material values.

Spirituality permeates, and ultimately subverts the ironic grit that hones the edge of Parker's report, without diminishing its worth or efficacy. Key images such as those four skulls, the solitary, majestically assured cactus, or the infinite Milky Way, not to mention the deliberately few, straightforward glimpses of the Lines themselves, serve to return us to a

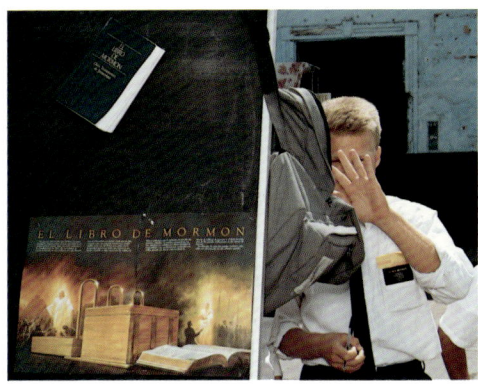

LATTER-DAY SAINT

universal centre. They affirm the power and pull of matters like myth, magic, archetype, and the collective unconscious.

Our undoubted fascination with the Lines portends a desire and marks a truth which requires constant reiteration in our contemporary 'use once and discard' society. Our spiritually impoverished civilisation piles up a cornucopia of rubbish tips, ecologically suspect middens waiting to be sifted by the archaeologists of the future, dressed in suitably protective clothing. If, that is, these treasure troves of domestic trivia have not been picked over first by the dispossessed of the present, in patently non-protective rags. A fine legacy indeed. Will the art museums of the future squabble for possession of the empty plastic petrol can, stamped with a crude, stereotyped image of a *campesina?*

However, our concern and anguish are perhaps warranted far more than our scorn. Parker's grimly humorous, chilling pile of discarded rubber gloves, like so many amputated limbs, reminds us sharply of more significant horrors. It reminds us of the tragic dimensions underscoring our morally deficient, increasingly rootless society — in which we have lost any clear sense of the past, and fail to find any confidence in the future. Such a profound dislocation generates feelings of emotional disengagement, and encourages social climates in which extremes might flourish. The alienated substrates of so many First World conurbations, or the political injustices of too much of the Third World, testify to that.

Throughout his narrative, by means of the telling juxtaposition, by utilising metaphor and allusion, not least the symbolic potency of the Lines themselves, Parker hints at these larger issues. He raises the questions, quietly declares his own viewpoint for those who wish to look, but his judgements are neither etched in stone nor declaimed in capital letters. David Parker certainly is a committed photographer, but he deliberately refrains from preaching. He questions, but does not deal out glib answers. His audience is allowed, indeed expected, to form its own conclusions.

Parker's own commitment is perhaps seen most clearly in his portraits. At first glance, they seem guardedly neutral, but in effect confer upon his subjects a grave and proper dignity, without being either cool or condescending. This neutrality functions as a positive force rather than states an absence of position. Parker refuses steadfastly to condemn the natives of Nazca for their indifference to the aesthetic efficacy of the Lines, for their understandable material acquisitiveness, or for their sullen animosity towards their conspicuously consuming tourist guests.

However, Parker is describing no stereotyped First versus Third World scenario, with victimising and victimised, good guys and bad guys. He might despair at the forces of history and politics which have created the different crises and needs within different societies, but his humanism offers some hope – though without the simplistic palliative of the easy answer. Parker also refuses to castigate the tourist outright, for have we not all been tourists at some point? We might claim for ourselves that there is a fine distinction between the traveller and the tourist mentally, nevertheless, we all know of the emptiness that tends to pervade the purely materialist existence, and can empathise with the desperate search for 'cultural' values, however inane or directionless its execution.

At a site like Nazca, we might see both native and visitor as victims – in differing degrees, certainly – but both flung together at the sharp end of the enormous, probably widening gulf between First and Third Worlds. That much is clear. The Lines, positive yet naturally discreet interventions in the landscape, evoke a slightly different dichotomy. They evoke that exquisite paradox, the immutable pull between man's inherent need to dominate the natural world and his desire for mystical merger with nature.

Thus Parker readily utilises the detached, intellectual side of his own psychological makeup to appreciate all the delicious ironies created when a community like Nazca writhes upon the horns of tourist colonisation. But that, in effect, would produce only half a book, or more precisely a book with only half the depth or breadth of Parker's. The dispassionate, even the too determinedly compassionate camera, is the ideal tool for such easy targets, and such glib, cliched contradictions. Nevertheless, they are cliched because they exist – they need to be taken, and pointed out. Parker has duly accomplished that side of his mission.

He has also completed the other, perhaps more ineffable, more difficult side of his task. He has succumbed himself, as I have iterated, to the magic of the Lines, and suggests another level of existence – effected, paradoxically, by means of the very intensity with which he has investigated the many facets of materialism in Nazca. Parker proposes that mystical participation in this world is potentially a viable state, notwithstanding the sheer crassness, spiritual poverty, and mundanity of the majority of contemporary values. Parker demonstrates that, in spite of their appropriation by all and sundry – tourists, archaeologists, occultists, garage owners, *campesinos* – the Lines remain strangely inviolate. Like the stupendous Colossi of Memnon in Egypt, which have been scrawled upon, shot at, hacked at, and are now surrounded by a pathetic fence of barbed wire, the Lines retain their dignity, their power, and their wonder.

The Nazca Lines are boundless and ultimately unknowable. Each pictograph is distinct and mute. The very act of their creation proclaims a living mystery, although the patient work of archaeologists has succeeded in largely defining their original cultural context. However, they remain, quite simply, works of art, using that much abused term in its widest, non-elitist, and most profound sense.

And David Parker's commentary upon them, and upon the present day community which surrounds them, is also a work of art, and as such, equally unknowable. So further commentary is probably superfluous. It is time to look – and ponder.

Lucy Lippard has stated that "art in society is nice but inconsequential." To be sure, perhaps art is small beer compared with the grand, tragic canvas of history, but inconsequential is surely the wrong term. The pull of the Nazca Lines, of Petra, or of the Temple of Karnak, suggests both consequence and a degree of necessity. Perhaps we merely should acknowledge that necessity without making either too much or too little of it. This, assuredly, is what David Parker has achieved in this eminently balanced, level headed, yet quietly impassioned study. He would surely agree with the recent words of Seamus Heaney. "Art is not to be applied glibly to society's wounds, like a poultice. Art is a palliative, not a cure."

Gerry Badger. January, 1991

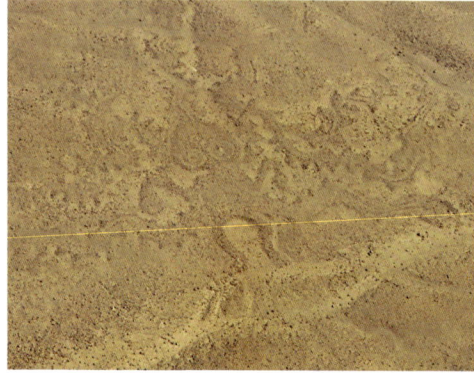

EMBRYO (E.T.)

ACKNOWLEDGEMENTS

All the photographs in this book were made in December '87, December '88 and August '89. During the course of this project many people gave me valuable help and support and I should like to take this opportunity to thank them all.

Firstly Jenny Ingham Clark for her tireless enthusiasm and energetic assistance during the gestation of *Broken Images*.

My brief meeting with Helaine Silverman in '88 was crucial to the evolution of the book's various themes. Her collaboration has been indispensible and at times inspirational. I am unable to thank her enough. Equally vital has been Gerry Badger's sustained interest and encouragement. His observations and insights have been invaluable in the shaping of this project.

I owe a debt of gratitude to Phyillis Pitluga for giving up many precious hours to accompany me onto the pampa, for her later contributions to the main text and for enlivening my stays in Nazca with her great charm and wit over many suppers.

Maria Reiche is of course the central figure in Nazca and I'm very grateful to her and to her sister Renate for their interest and assistance, particularly in helping on one occasion to turn Maria's hotel room into a portrait studio.

Also in Nazca I received help from Josue and Isabel Lancho, Teofilo Guia Ramos and my guides Marco and Armando.

Special thanks to Felicity Nock for the imaginative ideas she introduced into her editing of the main text. Also Dewi Lewis at Cornerhouse for his constant support and belief in this project, and Richard Adams for keeping my more grandiose ideas within the realms of the possible.

In addition I'd like to thank Tony Morrison and Gillian Marshall, Chairman and Treasurer respectively of the Anglo-Peruvian Society, for their support and assistance; Dr Carlos Zavaleta, Peruvian Cultural Attache, Federico Perez Eguren of FOPTUR (Lima) and Carmen Granda de Byrne of FOPTUR (London) for helping to smooth the way; Jennifer Kavanagh for her interest and advice; and Andy Jillings whose passion for Peru was the catalyst for my own involvement; and finally my beloved wife Jenny for being my second pair of eyes when I got so close to the work that I was furthest from my intuition.

David Parker 1991

DAVID PARKER

David Parker was born in 1949 in Stafford where he trained as an engineer. He first visited Peru in 1981 as a photographer on the Cusichaca Project, an archaeological dig near Machu Picchu. He now works freelance as a corporate and scientific photographer in London.

HELAINE SILVERMAN

Archaeologist Helaine Silverman was trained at Columbia University and the University of Texas at Austin from whence she received her doctoral degree in 1986. She has been conducting intensive archaeological excavations and surveys in the Nazca region since 1983. Dr. Silverman is the author of numerous scholarly articles on ancient Nasca culture. Her book, *Cahuachi in the Ancient Nasca World*, will be published by University of Iowa Press in 1992. Dr. Silverman is a member of the faculty of the Department of Anthropology at the University of Illinois at Urbana-Champaign.

GERRY BADGER

Gerry Badger is a photographer, writer and architect. he writes regularly on photographic matters and was co-curator of the recent exhibition of post-War British photography *Through the Looking Glass*, at the Barbican Art Gallery. His photographs are in public collections including the Museum of Modern Art, New York; the Biblioteque Nationale, Paris; and the V & A, London.

Gerry Badger expresses his thanks to Moris Farhi for the use of the title, 'The Spider Who Spins the Sky', taken from his novel, *Journey Through the Wilderness* (Macmillan, London 1990).